THE SCHOOL BOOK OF FORESTRY

CHARLES LATHROP PACK

PRESIDENT OF THE AMERICAN TREE ASSOCIATION

1st WORLD
LIBRARY
Literary Society

The Schoolbook of Forestry

Charles Lathrop Pack

© 1st World Library – Literary Society, 2005
PO Box 2211
Fairfield, IA 52556
www.1stworldlibrary.org
First Edition

LCCN: 2004195594

Softcover ISBN: 1-4218-0415-8
Hardcover ISBN: 1-4218-0315-1
eBook ISBN: 1-4218-0515-4

Purchase *"The Schoolbook of Forestry"*
as a traditional bound book at:
www.1stWorldLibrary.org/purchase.asp?ISBN=1-4218-0415-8

1st World Library Literary Society is a nonprofit
organization dedicated to promoting literacy by:

- Creating a free internet library accessible from any
  computer worldwide.
- Hosting writing competitions and offering book
  publishing scholarships.

The Schoolbook of Forestry
contributed by Tim, Ed & Rodney
in support of
1st World Library Literary Society

THE AUTHOR GRATEFULLY ACKNOWLEDGES INFORMATION AND ASSISTANCE FROM THE WRITINGS AND REPORTS OF COL. W.B. GREELEY, U.S. FORESTER; COL. HENRY S. GRAVES, FORMER U.S. FORESTER; GIFFORD PINCHOT, FORMER U.S. FORESTER; DR. B.E. FERNOW, DR. J.W. TOUMEY, F.W. BESLEY, W.I. HUTCHINSON, R.H.D. BOERKER, PROF. NELSON C. BROWN, PROF. R.S. HOSMER, E.A. STERLING, R.S. KELLOGG, E.T. ALLEN, S. GORDON DORRANCE, DR. HUGH P. BAKER, ALFRED GASKILL, J.S. ILLICK, AND MANY OTHER LEADERS IN FORESTRY.

"THE PART OF GOOD CITIZENS"

A people without children would face a hopeless future; a country without trees is almost as helpless; forests which are so used that they cannot renew themselves will soon vanish, and with them all their benefits. When you help to preserve our forests or plant new ones you are acting the part of good citizens.

THEODORE ROOSEVELT.

CONTENTS

INTRODUCTION

Our forests, with their billions of trees, are the backbone of agriculture, the skeleton of lumbering, and the heart of industry. Even now, in spite of their depletion, they are the cream of our natural resources. They furnish wood for the nation, pasture for thousands of cattle and sheep, and water supply for countless cities and farms. They are the dominions of wild life. Millions of birds, game animals, and fish live in the forests and the forest streams. The time is coming when our forests will be the greatest playgrounds of America. It is necessary that we preserve, protect, and expand our timberlands. By so doing we shall provide for the needs of future generations.

The forest is one of the most faithful friends of man. It provides him with materials to build homes. It furnishes fuel. It aids agriculture by preventing floods and storing the surplus rainfall in the soil for the use of farm crops. It supplies the foundation for all our railroads. It is the producer of fertile soils. It gives employment to millions of workmen. It is a resource which bountifully repays kind treatment. It is the best organized feature of the plant world. The forest is not merely a collection of different kinds of trees. It is a permanent asset which will yield large returns over long periods when properly managed.

Our forest fortune has been thoughtlessly squandered by successive generations of spendthrifts. Fortunately, it is not too late to rebuild it through cooeperative effort.

The work has been well begun, but it is a work of years, and it is to the youth of the country that we must look for its continuous expansion and perpetuation. A part of our effort must be directed toward familiarizing them with the needs and rewards of an intelligent forestry policy.

Charles Lathrop Pack

CHAPTER I

HOW TREES GROW AND MULTIPLY

The trees of the forest grow by forming new layers of wood directly under the bark. Trees are held upright in the soil by means of roots which reach to a depth of many feet where the soil is loose and porous. These roots are the supports of the tree. They hold it rigidly in position. They also supply the tree with food. Through delicate hairs on the roots, they absorb soil moisture and plant food from the earth and pass them along to the tree. The body of the tree acts as a passage way through which the food and drink are conveyed to the top or crown. The crown is the place where the food is digested and the regeneration of trees effected.

The leaves contain a material known as chlorophyll, which, in the presence of light and heat, changes mineral substances into plant food. Chlorophyll gives the leaves their green color. The cells of the plant that are rich in chlorophyll have the power to convert carbonic-acid gas into carbon and oxygen. These cells combine the carbon and the soil water into chemical mixtures which are partially digested when they reach the crown of the tree. The water, containing salts, which is gathered by the roots is brought up to the leaves. Here it combines with the carbonic-acid gas taken from the air. Under the action of chlorophyll and sunlight these substances are split up, the carbon, oxygen and hydrogen being combined into plant food. It is either used immediately or stored away for future emergency.

Trees breathe somewhat like human beings. They take in oxygen and give off carbonic-acid gas. The air enters the tree through the leaves and small openings in the bark, which are easily seen in such trees as the cherry and birch. Trees breathe constantly, but they digest and assimilate food only during the day and in the presence of light. In the process of digestion and assimilation they give off oxygen in abundance, but they retain most of the carbonic acid gas, which is a plant food, and whatever part of it is not used immediately is stored up by the tree and used for its growth and development. Trees also give off their excess moisture through the leaves and bark. Otherwise they would become waterlogged during periods when the water is rising rapidly from the roots.

After the first year, trees grow by increasing the thickness of the older buds. Increase in height and density of crown cover is due to the development of the younger twigs. New growth on the tree is spread evenly between the wood and bark over the entire body of the plant. This process of wood production resembles a factory enterprise in which three layers of material are engaged. In the first two of these delicate tissues the wood is actually made. The inner side of the middle layer produces new wood while the outer side grows bark. The third layer is responsible for the production of the tough, outer bark. Year after year new layers of wood are formed around the first layers. This first layer finally develops into heartwood, which, so far as growth is concerned, is dead material. Its cells

Charles Lathrop Pack

are blocked up and prevent the flow of sap. It aids in supporting the tree. The living sapwood surrounds the heartwood. Each year one ring of this sapwood develops. This process of growth may continue until the annual layers amount to 50 or 100, or more, according to the life of the tree.

One can tell the age of a tree by counting the number of annual rings. Sometimes, because of the interruption of normal growth, two false rings may be produced instead of a single true ring. However, such blemishes are easy for the trained eye to recognize. Heartwood does not occur in all varieties of trees. In some cases, where both heartwood and sapwood appear, it is difficult to distinguish between them as their colors are so nearly alike. Because it takes up so much moisture and plant food, sapwood rots much more quickly than heartwood. The sapwood really acts as a pipe line to carry water from the roots to the top of the tree. In some of our largest trees the moisture is raised as high as 300 feet or more through the sapwood.

Strange though it may seem, trees fight with each other for a place in the sunlight. Sprightly trees that shoot skyward at a swift pace are the ones that develop into the monarchs of the forest. They excel their mates in growth because at all times they are exposed to plenty of light. The less fortunate trees, that are more stocky and sturdy, and less speedy in their climb toward the sky, are killed out in large numbers each year. The weaker, spindly trees of the forest, which are slow growers, often are smothered out by the more vigorous trees.

Some trees are able to grow in the shade. They develop near or under the large trees of the forest. When the giants of the woodland die, these smaller trees, which previously were shaded, develop rapidly as a result of their freedom from suppression. In many cases they grow almost as large and high as the huge trees that they replace. In our eastern forests the hemlock often follows the white pine in this way. Spruce trees may live for many years in dense shade. Then finally, when they have access to plenty of light they may develop into sturdy trees. A tree that is a pigmy in one locality may rank as a giant in another region due to different conditions of growth and climate. For example, the canoe birch at its northern limit is a runt. It never grows higher than a few feet above the ground. Under the most favorable conditions in Florida, where this species thrives, such trees often tower to a height of 125 feet.

In sheltered regions the seeds of trees may fall, sprout and take root close to their parent trees. As a rule, the wind plays a prominent part in distributing seed in every section of the country. Pine and fir seeds are equipped with wings like those of a bird or an airplane. They enable the seeds to fly long distances on the wind before they drop to the ground and are covered with leaves. Maple seeds fly by means of double-winged sails which carry them far afield before they settle. Ash seeds have peculiar appendages which act like a skate-sail in transporting them to distant sections. Cotton-wood seeds have downy wings which aid their flight, while basswood seeds are distributed over the country by means of parachute-like wings. The pods of the locust tree fall on the frozen ground or snow crust and are blown long distances from their source. On the other hand, oak, hickory, and chestnut trees produce heavy seeds which generally remain where they fall.

Squirrels are the most industrious foresters in the animal world. Each year they bury great quantities of tree seeds in hoards or caches hidden away in hollow logs or in the moss and leaves of the forest floor. Birds also scatter tree seed here, there, and everywhere over the forests and the surrounding country. Running streams and rivers carry seeds uninjured for many miles and finally deposit them in places where they sprout and grow into trees. Many seeds are carried by the ocean currents to distant foreign shores.

The decay of leaves and woodland vegetation forms rich and fertile soils in the forests, in which conditions are favorable for the development of new tree growth. When living tree seeds are exposed to proper amounts of moisture, warmth and air in a fertile soil, they will sprout and grow. A root develops which pushes its way down into the soil, while the leaf-bud of the plant, which springs from the other end of the seed, works its way upward toward the light and air. This leafy part of the seed finally forms the stem of the tree. But trees may produce plenty of seed and yet fail to maintain their proper proportion in the forest. This results because much of the seed is unsound. Even where a satisfactory supply of sound fertile seed is produced, it does not follow that the trees of that variety will be maintained in the forest, as the seed supply may be scattered in unfavorable positions for germination. Millions of little seedlings, however, start to grow in the forest each year, but only a small number survive and become large trees. This is because so many of the seedlings are destroyed by forest fires, cattle and sheep grazing, unfavorable soil and weather conditions, and many other causes.

Beech and chestnut trees and others of the

broad-leaved type reproduce by means of sprouts as well as by seed. Generally, the young stumps of broad-leaved trees produce more sprouts than the stumps of older trees which have stood for some time. Among the cone-bearing trees reproduction by sprouts is rare. The redwood of California is one of the few exceptions. The pitch pine of the Eastern States produces many sprouts, few of which live and develop into marketable timber.

When trees are grown in nurseries, the practice is to sow the seed in special beds filled with rich soil. Lath screens are used as shade. They protect the young seedlings from the sun just as the parent trees would do in the forest. The seedbeds are kept well cultivated and free of weeds so that the seedlings may have the best opportunities for rapid growth. Generally the seeds are sown in the spring between March and May. Such seeds as the elms and soft maples, which ripen in the early summer, are sown as soon as possible after they are gathered. Practical tests have shown that thick sowings of tree seeds give the best results. There is little danger of weeds smothering out the seedlings under such conditions. After the seed has germinated the beds may be thinned so that the seedlings will have more room to develop.

During the fall of the same year, or in the following spring, the seedlings should be transplanted to nursery rows. Thereafter it is customary to transplant the young trees at least once again during damp weather. When the trees finally are robust and vigorous and have reached the age of two to five years, they are dug up carefully and set out permanently. The usual practice is to keep the seedlings one year in the seedbed and two years in the nursery rows before they are set out.

Charles Lathrop Pack

Whether the transplanting should take place during the spring or fall depends largely on the climate and geography of the locality. Practical experience is the best guide in such matters.

Some farmers and land owners are now interested in setting out hardwood forests for commercial purposes. If they do not wish to purchase their seedlings from a reliable nursery-man, they can grow them from carefully selected seed planted in well-prepared seedbeds. The popular practice is to sow the seed in drills about 2 to 3 feet apart so that horses may be used for cultivation. The seeds are sown to a depth of 2 to 3 times their thickness. They are placed close enough in the drill so that from 12 to 15 seedlings to the linear foot result. In order to hasten the sprouting of the seeds, some planters soak them in cold water for several days before sowing. In the case of such hard-coated seed as the black locust or honey locust, it is best to soak them in hot water before planting.

CHAPTER II

THE FOREST FAMILIES

Trees are as queer in picking out places to live and in their habits of growth as are the peoples of the various races which inhabit the world. Some trees do best in the icy northland. They become weak and die when brought to warm climates. Others that are accustomed to tropical weather fail to make further growth when exposed to extreme cold. The appearance of Jack Frost means death to most of the trees that come from near the equator. Even on the opposite slopes of the same mountain the types of trees are often very different. Trees that do well on the north side require plenty of moisture and cool weather. Those that prosper on south exposures are equipped to resist late and early frosts as well as very hot sunshine. The moisture needs of different trees are as remarkable as their likes and dislikes for warmth and cold. Some trees attain large size in a swampy country. Trees of the same kind will become stunted in sections where dry weather persists.

In some parts of the United States forestry experts can tell where they are by the local tree growth. For example, in the extreme northern districts the spruce and the balsam fir are native. As one travels farther south these give way to little Jack pine and aspen trees. Next come the stately forests of white and Norway

Charles Lathrop Pack

pine. Sometimes a few slow-growing hemlock trees appear in the colder sections. If one continues his journey toward the equator he will next pass through forests of broad-leaved trees. They will include oak, maple, beech, chestnut, hickory, and sycamore.

In Kentucky, which is a centre of the broad-leaved belt, there are several hundred different varieties of trees. Farther south, the cone-bearing species prevail. They are followed in the march toward the Gulf of Mexico by the tropical trees of southern Florida. If one journeys west from the Mississippi River across the Great Plains he finally will come to the Rocky Mountains, where evergreen trees predominate. If oak, maple, poplar, or other broad-leaved trees grow in that region, they occur in scattered stands. In the eastern forests the trees are close together. They form a leafy canopy overhead. In the forests of the Rockies the evergreens stand some distance apart so that their tops do not touch. As a result, these Western forests do not shade the ground as well as those in the east. This causes the soils of these forests to be much drier, and also increases the danger from fire.

The forests of western Washington and Oregon, unlike most timberlands of the Rocky Mountain Region, are as dense as any forests in the world. Even at midday it is as dark as twilight in these forests. The trees are gigantic. They tower 150 to 300 feet above the ground. Their trunks often are 6 feet or larger in diameter. They make the trees of the eastern forests look stunted. They are excelled in size only by the mammoth redwood trees of northern California and the giant Sequoias of the southern Sierras.

Differences of climate have largely influenced tree

growth and types in this country. The distribution of tree families is changing all the time. It shifts just as the climate and other conditions change. Trees constantly strive among themselves for control of different localities. For a time one species will predominate. Then other varieties will appear and displace the ones already established. The distribution of trees changes very remarkably from one century to another. For example, in some sections, the red and black oaks are replacing the white oaks. Some trees are light-lovers. They require much more sunlight than others that do well under heavy shade. Oak trees require plenty of light; maples or beeches thrive on little light.

The seed of trees requiring little light may be scattered in a dense forest together with that of trees which need plenty of daylight in order to make normal growth. The seedlings that like shade will develop under such conditions while those that need light will pine away and die. Gradually the shade-loving trees will replace the light-loving trees in such a forest stand. Even the different trees of the same family often strive with one another for light and moisture. Each tree differs from every other one in shape and size. Trees will adapt themselves to the light and moisture conditions to which they are exposed. A tree that has access to plenty of moisture and sunlight grows evenly from the ground to its top with a bushy, wide-spreading crown. The same tree, if it grows in the shade, will reach a greater height but will have a small compact crown. Trees run a race in their rapidity of growth. The winners get the desirable places in the sunlight and prosper. The losers develop into stunted trees that often die, due to lack of light exposure. A better quality of lumber results from tall straight trees than that produced by the symmetrical, branching trees. That is

Charles Lathrop Pack

why every forester who sets out trees tries to provide conditions which will make them grow tall and with the smallest possible covering of branches on the lower part of the trunks.

Where trees are exposed to strong winds, they develop deep and strong root systems. They produce large and strong trunks that can bend and resist violent winds which sway and twist them in every direction. Such trees are much stronger and sturdier than those that grow in a sheltered forest. The trees that are blown down in the forest provide space for the introduction and growth of new varieties. These activities are constantly changing the type of tree growth in the forest.

Our original forests which bordered the Atlantic coast line when America was first settled, were dense and impenetrable. The colonists feared the forests because they sheltered the hostile Indians who lurked near the white settlements. In time this fear of the forest developed into hatred of the forest. As a result, the colonists cut trees as rapidly as they could. In every way they fought back the wilderness. They and their children's children have worked so effectively that the original wealth of woodlands has been depleted. At present, cleared fields and cutover areas abound in regions that at one time were covered with magnificent stands of timber.

In many sections of the country our forests are now so reduced that they are of little commercial importance. However, these areas are not yet entirely denuded. Predictions have been made frequently that our woodlands would soon disappear. Scientific foresters report that such statements are incorrect. There are only a few districts in the country which probably will never again support much tree growth. Their denuded condition is due largely to the destruction of the neighboring mountain forests and to the activities of erosion. Under ordinary conditions, natural reforestation will maintain a satisfactory tree growth on lands where a practical system of forest protection is practiced. The complete removal of the forest is now accomplished only in fertile farming regions, where the agricultural value of the land is too high to permit it to remain longer in forest cover. Even in the Mississippi Valley and the Great Lakes belts there are still large areas of forest land. Most of the farms have woodlots which provide fuel, fencing, and some lumber. For the most part, these farm woodlots are abused. They have not been managed correctly. Fortunately, a change for the better is now evident. The farm woodlot owners are coming to appreciate the importance of protecting the trees for future use. In some cases, they are even replanting areas that have been cut over. There are large tracts of sandy, rocky and swampy land in these districts that are satisfactory for tree production. In fact, about all these fields are good for is the growing of timber. Campaigns are now under way to increase tree planting and develop the production of lands adapted for forestry which previously have been idle.

The United States of the future will not be a desert, tree-less country. However, immediate measures to save our remaining trees must be developed. The greater part of our virgin timber has already been felled. The aftermath forests, which succeed the virgin stand, generally are inferior. Our supplies of ash, black walnut and hickory, once abundant, are now seriously limited. Formerly, these mixed forests covered vast

Charles Lathrop Pack

stretches of country which today support only a scant crop of young trees which will not be ready for market for many years. These second-growth stands will never approach in value or quality the original forests. Over large areas, poplar, white birch, and Jack pine trees now predominate on lands which formerly bore dense stands of white pine. In many places, scrubby underbrush and stunted trees occupy lands which heretofore have been heavy producers of marketable timber trees.

Generally speaking, farm lands should not be used for forestry purposes. On the other hand, some forest lands can be profitably cleared and used for agriculture. For example, settlers are felling trees and fighting stumps in northern Wisconsin, Michigan, and Minnesota. Some of these virgin lands are valuable for farming purposes, others are not. It is preferable that they should produce farm crops instead of tree crops if the land is best adapted to agricultural use. It is an economic necessity that all lands in this country best suited for farming purposes should be tilled. Our ever-increasing population demands that every acre of land useful for growing crops should be cleared and devoted to farming. Under such conditions, the settlers should reserve sufficient woodlands for their home needs, carefully distinguishing between the land that is best for agricultural purposes and the land that is best for forestry purposes, and thus doubling their resources.

Thoughtless lumbermen have pillaged millions of acres of our most productive forests. The early lumbermen wasted our woodland resources. They made the same mistakes as everyone else in the care and protection of our original forests. The greatest blame for the wasting of our lumber resources rests with the

State and Federal authorities who permitted the depletion. Many of our lumbermen now appreciate the need of preserving and protecting our forests for future generations. Some of them have changed their policies and are now doing all in their power to aid forest conservation.

The ability of a properly managed forest to produce new crops of trees year after year promises us a future supply of wood sufficient for all our needs if only we will conserve our timberlands as they deserve. It is our duty to handle the forests in the same way that fertile farming fields are managed. That is to say, they should be so treated that they will yield a profitable money crop every year without reducing their powers of future production. Private owners and farmers are coming slowly to realize the grave importance of preserving and extending our woodlands. The public, the State and the Nation are now solidly behind the movement to improve our forestry and to safe-guard our forests. Several of the States, including New York and Pennsylvania, have purchased large areas of timberlands for State forests. These will be developed as future sources of lumber supply.

CHAPTER III

FORESTS AND FLOODS

Forests are necessary at the headwaters of streams. The trees break the force of the rain drops, and the forest floor, acting as a large sponge, absorbs rainfall and prevents run-off and floods. Unless there are forests at the sources of streams and rivers, floods occur. The spring uprisings of the Mississippi, Ohio and Missouri Rivers are due largely to the lack of forests at their headwaters. In the regions drained by these streams the run-off water is not absorbed as it should be. It flows unimpeded from the higher levels to the river valleys. It floods the river courses with so much water that they burst their banks and pour pell-mell over the surrounding country. Many floods which occur in the United States occur because we have cut down large areas of trees which formerly protected the sources of streams and rivers.

A grave danger that threatens western farming is that some time in the future the greater part of the vegetation and forest cover on the watersheds of that section may entirely disappear. Such a condition would cause floods after every heavy rain. The available supplies of rainwater which are needed for the thirsty crops would be wasted as flood waters. These floods would cause great damage in the valleys through which they rushed. The freshets would be followed by periods of water famine. The streams would then be so low that they could not supply the normal demands. Farmers would suffer on account of the lack of irrigation water. Towns and cities that depended on the mountain streams for their water supplies would be handicapped severely. In a thousand and one ways, a deficient water supply due to forest depletion would cause hardships and suffering in the regions exposed to such misfortune.

The important part which forests play in the development of our country is shown by the fact that from the streams of the National Forests over 700 western cities and towns, with an aggregate population of nearly 2,500,000, obtain their domestic water supply. The forests include 1266 irrigation projects and 325 water-power plants, in addition to many other power and irrigation companies which depend on the Government timberlands for water conservation and the regulation of rain water run-off and stream flow.

The National Forests aid greatly in conserving and making available for use the precious limited rainfall of the arid regions. That is why settlers in irrigated districts are deeply interested in the cutting of timber in the Federal woodlands. Destructive lumbering is never practiced in these forests. In its place has been substituted a system of management that assures the continued preservation of the forest-cover. Uncle Sam is paying special attention to the western water-sheds which supply reclamation and irrigation projects. He understands that the ability of the forest to regulate stream flow is of great importance. The irrigation farmers also desire a regular flow, evenly distributed, throughout the growing season.

One of the chief reasons for the establishment of the National Forest was to preserve the natural conditions favorable to stream flow. In a treeless country, the rise of the streams is a very accurate measure of the rainfall. In the region where forests are frequent, an ordinary rain is scarcely noticed in its effect on the stream. In a denuded district no natural obstacles impede the raindrops as they patter to the ground. The surface of the soil is usually hard. It is baked and dried out by the sun. It is not in condition to absorb or retain much of the run-off water, consequently, the rain water finds little to stop it as it swirls down the slopes. In torrents it rushes down the stream beds, like sheets of water flowing down the steep roof of a house.

Conditions are very different in a region where forest cover is abundant. In the forests, the tops of the trees catch much of the rain that falls. The leaves, twigs, branches and trunks of the trees also soak up considerable moisture. The amount of rainfall that directly strikes the ground is relatively small. The upper layer of the forested ground consists of a network of shrubs, and dead leaves, branches, and moss. This forest carpet acts like an enormous sponge. It soaks up the moisture which drops from the trees during a storm. It can absorb and hold for a time a rainfall of four or five inches. The water that finally reaches the ground sinks into the soil and is evaporated or runs off slowly. The portion that is absorbed by the soil is taken up by the roots of the trees and plants or goes to supply springs and watercourses.

The power of the trees and forest soil to absorb water regulates the rate at which the rainfall is fed to the streams and rivers. Frequently it takes weeks and even months for all the waters of a certain rain to reach these streams. This gradual supplying of water to the streams regulates their flow. It prevents floods and freshets. Careful observation and measurements have shown that unforested regions will discharge rain water at least twice as fast as will forested districts.

The stealing of soil by erosion occurs where run-off waters are not obstructed by forest growth. Silt, sand, and every other kind of soil are swept from their natural positions and spritted away by the foaming waters as they surge down the steep slopes. The stream or river which is flooded by these rushing waters roars down its narrow channel, tearing loose and undermining the jutting banks. In some cases, it will break from its ordinary course to flood exposed fields and to carry away more soil. As the speed of the stream increases its power to steal soil and carry it off is increased. Engineers report that the carrying power of a stream is increased 64 times when its rate of flow is doubled. If the flow of a river is speeded up ten times, this raging torrent will be able to carry one million times as much foreign material as it did when it was flowing at a normal rate of speed, causing inexpressible damage and destruction of life and property.

The protection afforded by forests on the water-sheds of streams furnishing the domestic water supply for cities and towns is becoming more fully realized. A large number of cities and towns have purchased and are maintaining municipal or communal forests for this very reason.

CHAPTER IV

WILD LIFE OF THE FOREST

The forests of our country are the home and breeding grounds of hundreds of millions of birds and game animals, which the forests provide with food and shelter. If we had no forests, many of these birds and animals would soon disappear. The acorns and other nuts that the squirrels live upon are examples of the food that the forest provides for its residents.

In the clear, cold streams of the forests there are many different kinds of fish. If the forests were destroyed by cutting or fire many of the brooks and rivers would either dry up or the water would become so low that thousands of fish would die.

The most abundant game animals of forest regions are deer, elk, antelope and moose. Partridge, grouse, quail, wild turkeys and other game birds are plentiful in some regions. The best known of all the inhabitants of the woods are the squirrels. The presence of these many birds and animals adds greatly to the attractiveness of the forest.

Predatory animals, such as wolves, bears, mountain lions, coyotes and bobcats also live in the forest. They kill much livestock each year in the mountain regions of the Western States and they also prey on some species of bird life. The Federal and some State governments now employ professional hunters to trap and shoot these marauders. Each year the hunters kill thousands of predatory animals, thus saving the farmers and cattle and sheep owners many thousands of dollars.

Sportsmen are so numerous and hunting is so popular, that game refuges have to be provided in the forests and parks. Were it not for these havens of refuge where hunting is not permitted, some of our best known wild game and birds would soon be extinct. There are more than 11,640,648 acres of forest land in the government game refuges. California has 22 game refuges in her 17 National Forests. New Mexico has 19, while Montana, Idaho, Colorado, Washington and Oregon also have set aside areas of government forest land for that purpose. In establishing a game refuge, it is necessary to pick out a large area of land that contains enough good feed for both the summer and winter use of the animals that will inhabit it.

Livestock is sometimes grazed on game refuges, but only in small numbers, so that plenty of grass will be left for the support of the wild game. The refuges are under the direction of the Federal and the State game departments. To perpetuate game animals and game birds, it is not enough to pass game laws and forbid the shooting of certain animals and birds except at special times of the year; it is also necessary to provide good breeding grounds for the birds and animals where they will not be molested or killed. The game refuges provide such conditions.

The division of the range country into small farms and

the raising of all kinds of crops have, it is claimed, done more to decrease our herds of antelope, elk, deer and other big game than have the rifles of the hunters. The plow and harrow have driven the wild life back into the rougher country. The snow becomes very deep in the mountains in the winter and the wild animals could not get food were it not for the game refuges in the low country. In the Yellowstone National Park country great bands of elk come down from the mountains during severe winters and have to be fed on hay to keep them from starving, as there is not sufficient winter range in this region to supply food for the thousands of elk.

Where the elk are protected from hunters they increase rapidly. This means that some of the surplus animals have to be killed, otherwise, the elk would soon be so numerous that they would seriously interfere with the grazing of domestic livestock. In different sections of the elk country, a count is made every few years on the breeding animals in each band. Whenever a surplus accumulates, the state permits hunters to shoot some of the elk. If the breeding herds get too small, no hunting is allowed. In this way, a proper balance is maintained.

In many states the wild game birds and fur-bearing animals of the forests are protected by closed seasons during which hunting is not permitted. It is realized that birds and animals are not only of interest to visitors to the forests, but that they, as well as the trees, are a valuable forest product.

CHAPTER V

IMPORTANT FOREST TREES AND THEIR USES

Of our native trees, the white pine is one of the best and most valuable. It is a tall straight tree that grows to a height of 100 to 150 feet. It produces wood that is light in weight and easy to work because it is so soft. At one time there were extensive pine forests in the northeastern states. Many of the trees were very large, and occasionally one may still see pine stumps that are 5 to 6 feet in diameter. White pine made fine lumber for houses and other buildings and this timber was among the first to be exhausted in the country.

Spruce trees have long furnished the bulk of the woodpulp used in making our supplies of paper. These trees live in the colder climates of the northern states. They like to grow in low, wet localities close to lakes or rivers. The spruces generally do not grow higher than 75-100 feet. The wood is soft like pine and even whiter in color. The aboriginal Indians used the roots of the spruce trees as thread, twine and rope.

The cedar trees, which are landmarks in many of our northern states, yield light, soft, durable wood that is useful in making poles, fence posts, lead pencils and cedar chests. The wood of the red cedar gives off a peculiar odor which is said to keep moths away from clothes stored in cedar chests, but it is the close construction of the chest which keeps them out. These trees are becoming scarce in all parts of the country. Cedars generally are small trees that grow slowly and live a long time. The outside wood is white and the heartwood is red or yellow. Cedar posts last a long time and are excellent for use in farm fences.

Chestnut blight, which destroys entire forests of chestnut timber, is gradually exhausting our supplies of this wood. Chestnut timber has long been used for railroad ties, fence posts and in the manufacture of cheap furniture. The wood is soft and brown in color. The bark and wood are treated at special plants in such a way that an extract which is valuable for tanning leather is obtained. Chestnut trees are upstanding, straight trees that tower 80 to 100 feet above the ground. The extinction of our chestnut forests threatens as no effectual control measures for checking the chestnut blight disease over large areas has yet been discovered.

The yellow poplar or tulip poplar furnishes timber for the manufacture of furniture, paper, the interior of railroad cars and automobiles. The dugouts of the early settlers and Indians were hewed out of poplar logs. These boats were stronger than those made of canoe birch. Poplar wood is yellow in color and soft in texture. The poplar is the largest broad-leaf tree in this country and the trees are of great size and height. Some specimens found in the mountains of the South have been over 200 feet high and 8 to 10 feet in diameter, while poplars 125 to 150 feet high are quite common.

Among our most useful and valuable trees are the white oak, and its close kin, the red oak, which produce a brown-colored, hard wood of remarkable durability. The white oak is the monarch of the forest, as it lives very long and is larger and stronger than the majority of its associates. The timber is used for railroad ties, furniture, and in general construction work where tough, durable lumber is needed. Many of our wooden ships have been built of oak. The white oaks often grow as high as 100 feet and attain massive dimensions. The seeds of the white oaks are light brown acorns, which are highly relished by birds and animals. Many southern farmers range their hogs in white oak forests so that the porkers can live on the acorn crop.

Beech wood is strong and tough and is used in making boxes and barrels and casks for the shipment of butter, sugar and other foods. It makes axles and shafts for water-wheels that will last for many years. The shoes worn by Dutch children are generally made of beech. The wood is red in color. The beech tree is of medium size growing to a height of about 75 feet above the ground. There is only one common variety of beech tree in this country.

Hickory trees are very popular because they produce sweet, edible nuts. The hickory wood is exceedingly strong and tough and is used wherever stout material is needed. For the spokes, wheels and bodies of buggies and wagons, for agricultural implements, for auto-mobile wheels and for handles, hickory is unexcelled. The shafts of golf clubs as well as some types of base-ball bats are made of hickory. Most hickory trees are easy to identify on account of their shaggy bark. The nuts of the hickory, which ripen in the autumn, are sweet, delicious and much in demand.

Our native elm tree is stately, reaching a height of 100 feet and a diameter of 5 to 6 feet or more. It is one of our best shade trees. Elm wood is light brown in color and very heavy and strong. It is the best available wood for making wagon wheel hubs and is also used largely for baskets and barrels. The rims of bicycle wheels generally are made of elm.

The canoe birch is a tree which was treasured by the early Indians because it yielded bark for making canoes. Birch wood is used in making shoe lasts and pegs because of its strength and light weight, and the millions of spools on which cotton is wound are made of birch wood. School desks and church furniture, also, are made of birch. The orange-colored inner bark of the birch tree is so fine and delicate that the early settlers could use it as they would paper. No matter whether birch wood is green or dry, it will burn readily. The birch was the most useful tree of the forest to the Indians. Its bark was used not only for making their canoes, but also for building their wigwams. They even dried and ground the inner bark into a flour which they used as a food.

The northern sugar maple is another tree which is a favorite in all sections where it is grown. This tree yields a hard wood that is the best and toughest timber grown in some localities. The trees grow to heights of 75 to 100 feet and attain girths of 5 to 9 feet. Maple lumber is stout and heavy. It makes fine flooring and is used in skating rinks and for bowling alleys. Many pianos are made of maple. Wooden dishes and rolling pins are usually made from maple wood. During the spring of the year when the sap is flowing, the average mature maple tree will yield from fifteen to twenty gallons of sap in a period of three to four weeks. This sap is afterwards boiled down to maple syrup and sugar.

Hemlock trees, despite the fact that they rank among the most beautiful trees of the forest, produce lumber which is suitable only for rough building operations. The wood is brown and soft and will not last long when exposed to the weather. It cracks and splits easily because it is so brittle. Hemlock is now of considerable importance as pulpwood for making paper. For many years, a material important for tanning leather has been extracted in large amounts from the bark of hemlock trees.

One of the most pleasing uses to which the balsam fir is put is as Christmas trees. Sometimes it is used in making paper pulp. The balsam fir seldom grows higher than 50 feet or thicker than 12 inches. The leaves of this tree have a very sweet odor and are in demand at Christmas time. Foresters and woodsmen often use balsam boughs to make their beds and pillows when camping in the woods.

Our native supplies of hardwoods and softwoods are used for general building purposes, for farm repairs, for railroad ties, in the furniture and veneer industry, in the handle industry, and in the vehicle and agricultural implement industries. On the average each American farmer uses about 2,000 board feet of lumber each year. New farm building decreased in the several years following the World War, due to the high price of lumber and labor. As a result of this lack of necessary building, millions of dollars worth of farm machinery stood out in the weather. Livestock lacked stables in some sections. Very little building was done in that period in two hundred and fifty prosperous agricultural counties in thirty-two different states.

The railroads consume about 15 per cent. of our total lumber cut. They use between 100,000,000 and 125,000,000 railroad ties a year. It used to be that most of the cross-ties were of white oak cut close to the places where they were used. Now Douglas fir, southern pine and other woods are being used largely throughout the Middle Western and Eastern States. The supply of white oak ties is small and the prices are high. Some years ago, when white oak was abundant, the railroads that now are using other cross-ties would not have even considered such material for use in their roadbeds. The fact that other ties are now being used emphasizes the fact that we are short on oak timber in the sections where this hardwood formerly was common.

The furniture industry uses hardwoods of superior grade and quality. The factories of this industry have moved from region to region as the supply of hardwoods became depleted. Originally, these factories were located in the Northeastern States. Then, as the supplies of hardwood timber in those sections gave out, they moved westward. They remained near the Corn Belt until the virgin hardwood forests of the Middle West were practically exhausted. The furniture industry is now largely dependent on what hardwoods are left in the remote sections of the Southern Appalachians and the lower Mississippi Valley. When these limited supplies are used up, there will be very little more old-growth timber in the country for them to use.

The furniture, veneer, handle, vehicle, automobile and agricultural implement industries all are in competition for hardwood timber. The furniture industry uses 1,250,000,000 feet of high-grade hardwood lumber annually. Production of timber of this type for furniture has decreased as much as 50 per cent. during the past few years. It is now difficult for the furniture factories and veneer plants to secure enough raw materials. Facilities for drying the green lumber artificially are few. It used to be that the hardwood lumber was seasoned for six to nine months before being sold. Furniture dealers now have to buy the material green from the sawmills. Competition has become so keen that buyers pay high prices. They must have the material to keep their plants running and to supply their trade.

The veneer industry provides furniture manufacturers, musical instrument factories, box makers and the automobile industry with high-grade material. The industry uses annually 780,000,000 board feet of first quality hardwood cut from virgin stands of timber. Red gum and white oak are the hardwoods most in demand. In the Lake States, a branch of the veneer industry which uses maple, birch and basswood is located. Oak formerly was the most important wood used. Now red gum has replaced the oak, as the supplies of the latter timber have dwindled. At present there is less than one-fourth of a normal supply of veneer timber in sight. Even the supplies in the farmers' woodlands are being depleted. The industry is now largely dependent on the timber of the southern Mississippi Valley. The veneer industry requires best-grade material. Clear logs are demanded that are at least 16 inches in diameter at the small end. It is getting harder every year to secure such logs. Like the furniture industry, the veneer mills lack adequate supplies of good timber.

No satisfactory substitutes for the hickory and ash used in the handle industry have yet been found. About the only stocks of these timbers now left are in the Southern States. Even in those parts the supplies are getting short and it is necessary to cut timber in the more remote sections distant from the railroad. The ash shortage is even more serious than that of hickory timber. The supplies of ash in the Middle West States north of the Ohio River are practically exhausted. The demand for ash and hickory handles is larger even than before the World War. The entire world depends on the United States for handles made from these woods. Handle dealers are now willing to pay high prices for ash and hickory timber. Some of them prepared for the shortage by buying tracts of hardwood timber. When these reserves are cut over, these dealers will be in the same position as the rest of the trade.

Ash and hickory are in demand also by the vehicle and agricultural implement industries. They also use considerable oak and compete with the furniture industry to secure what they need of this timber. Most of these plants are located in the Middle West but they draw their timber chiefly from the South. Hickory is a necessary wood to the vehicle industry for use in spokes and wheels. The factories exert every effort to secure adequate supplies of timber from the farm woodlands, sawmills and logging camps. The automobile industry now uses considerable hickory in the wheels and spokes of motor cars.

Most of the stock used by the vehicle industry is purchased green. Neither the lumber nor vehicle industry is equipped with enough kilns for curing this green material. The losses in working and manufacturing are heavy, running as high as 40 per cent. Many substitutes for ash, oak and hickory have been tried but they have failed to prove satisfactory. On account of the shortage and the high prices of hickory, vehicle factories are using steel in place of hickory wherever possible. Steel is more expensive but it can always be secured in quantity when needed. Furthermore, it is durable and very strong.

Thus we see that our resources of useful soft woods and hard woods have both been so diminished that prompt reforestation of these species is an urgent necessity.

CHAPTER VI

THE GREATEST ENEMY OF THE FOREST - FIRE

Our forests are exposed to destruction by many enemies, the worst of which is fire. From 8,000,000 to 12,000,000 acres of forest lands annually are burned over by destructive fires. These fires are started in many different ways. They may be caused by sparks or hot ashes from a locomotive. Lightning strikes in many forests every summer, particularly those of the Western States, and ignites many trees. In the South people sometimes set fires in order to improve the grazing. Settlers and farmers who are clearing land often start big brush fires that get out of their control. Campers, tourists, hunters, and fishermen are responsible for many forest fires by neglecting to extinguish their campfires. Sparks from logging engines also cause fires. Cigar and cigarette stubs and burning matches carelessly thrown aside start many forest fires. Occasionally fires are also maliciously set by evil-minded people.

The officers of the National Forests in the West have become very expert in running down the people who set incendiary fires. They collect evidence at the scene of the fire, such as pieces of letters and envelopes, matches, lost handkerchiefs and similar articles. They hunt for foot tracks and hoof marks. They study automobile tire tracks. They make plaster of Paris impressions of these tracks. They follow the tracks - sometimes Indian fashion. Often there are peculiarities about the tracks which lead to the detection and punishment of the culprits. A horse may be shod in an unusual manner; a man may have peculiar hob nails or rubber heels on his boots or else his footprints may show some deformity. The forest rangers play the parts of detectives very well. This novel police work has greatly reduced the number of incendiary fires.

A forest fire may destroy in a few hours trees that required hundreds of years to grow. A heavy stand of timber may be reduced to a desolate waste because some one forgot to put out a campfire. Occasionally large forest fires burn farm buildings and homes and kill hundreds of people. During the dry summer season when a strong wind is blowing, the fire will run for many miles. It always leaves woe and desolation in its wake. A mammoth forest fire in Wisconsin many years ago burned over an area of two thousand square miles. It killed about fourteen hundred people and destroyed many millions of dollars worth of timber and other property. A big forest fire in Michigan laid waste a tract forty miles wide and one hundred and eighty miles long. More than four billion feet of lumber, worth $10,000,000, was destroyed and several hundred people lost their lives. In recent years, a destructive forest fire in Minnesota caused a loss of $25,000,000 worth of timber and property.

There are several different kinds of forest fires. Some burn unseen two to four feet beneath the surface of the ground. Where the soil contains much peat, these fires may persist for weeks or even months. Sometimes, they do not give off any noticeable smoke. Their fuel is the decaying wood, tree roots and similar material in the soil. These underground fires can be stopped only by flooding the area or by digging trenches down to the mineral soil. The most effectual way to fight light surface fires is to throw sand or earth on the flames. Where the fire has not made much headway, the flames can sometimes be beaten out with green branches, wet gunny sacks or blankets. The leaves and debris may be raked away in a path so as to impede their advance.

Usually in the hardwood forests, there is not much cover, such as dry leaves, on the ground. Fires in these forests destroy the seedlings and saplings, but do not usually kill the mature trees. However, they damage the base of the trees and make it easy for fungi and insects to enter. They also burn the top soil and reduce the water-absorbing powers of the forest floor. In thick, dense evergreen forests where the carpet is heavy, fires are much more serious. They frequently kill the standing trees, burning trunks and branches and even following the roots deep into the ground. Dead standing trees and logs aid fires of this kind. The wind sweeps pieces of burning bark or rotten wood great distances to kindle new fires. When they fall, dead trees scatter sparks and embers over a wide belt. Fires also run along the tops of the coniferous trees high above the ground. These are called "crown-fires" and are very difficult to control.

The wind plays a big part in the intensity of a forest fire. If the fire can be turned so that it will run into the wind, it can be put out more easily. Fires that have the wind back of them and plenty of dry fuel ahead, speed on their way of destruction at a velocity of 5 to 10 miles an hour, or more. They usually destroy everything in their course that will burn, and waste great amounts of valuable timber. Wild animals, in panic, run together before the flames. Settlers and farmers with their families flee. Many are overtaken in the mad flight and perish. The fierce fires of this type can be stopped only by heavy rain, a change of wind, or by barriers which provide no fuel and thus choke out the flames.

Large fires are sometimes controlled by back-firing. A back-fire is a second fire built and so directed as to run against the wind and toward the main fire. When the two fires meet, both will go out on account of lack of fuel. When properly used by experienced persons, back-fires are very effectual. In inexperienced hands they are dangerous, as the wind may change suddenly or they may be lighted too soon. In such cases they often become as great a menace as the main fire. Another practical system of fighting fires is to make fire lines around the burning area. These fire lines or lanes as they are sometimes called, are stretches of land from which all trees and shrubs have been removed. In the centre of the lines a narrow trench is dug to mineral soil or the lines are plowed or burned over so that they are bare of fuel. Such lines also are of value around woods and grain fields to keep the fire out. They are commonly used along railroad tracks where locomotive sparks are a constant source of fire dangers.

Our forests, on account of their great size and the relatively small man force which guards them, are more exposed to fire dangers than any other woodlands in the world. The scant rainfall of many of the western states where great unbroken areas of forest are located increases the fire damages. The fact that the western country in many sections is sparsely settled favors destruction by forest fires. The prevalence of lightning in the mountains during the summer adds farther to the danger. One of the most important tasks of the rangers in the Federal forests is to prevent forest fires.

During the fire season, extra forest guards are kept busy hunting for signs of smoke throughout the forests. The lookouts in their high towers, which overlook large areas of forest, watch constantly for smoke, and as soon as they locate signs of fire they notify the supervisor of the forest. Lookouts use special scientific instruments which enable them to locate the position of the fires from the smoke. At the supervisor's head-quarters and the ranger stations scattered through the forests, equipment, horses and automobiles are kept ready for instant use when a fire is reported. Telephone lines and radio sets are used to spread the news about fires that have broken out.

From five thousand to six thousand forest fires occur each year in the National Forests of our country. To show how efficient the forest rangers are in fighting fires, it is worthy of note that by their prompt actions, 80 per cent. of these fires are confined to areas of less than ten acres each, while only 20 per cent. spread over areas larger than ten acres. Lightning causes from 25 to 30 per cent. of the fires. The remaining 70 or 75 per cent. are classed as "man-caused fires," which are set by campers, smokers, railroads, brush burners, sawmills and incendiaries. The total annual loss from forest fires in the Federal forests varies from a few hundred thousands of dollars in favorable years to several million in particularly bad fire seasons. During the last few years, due to efficient fire-fighting methods, the annual losses have been steadily reduced.

The best way of fighting forest fires is to prevent them. The forest officers do their best to reduce the chances for fire outbreak in the Government woodlands. They give away much dead timber that either has fallen or still is standing. Lumbermen who hold contracts to cut timber in the National Forest are required to pile and burn all the slashings. Dry grass is a serious fire menace. That is why grazing is encouraged in the forests. Rangers patrol the principal automobile roads to see that careless campers and tourists have not left burning campfires. Railroads are required to equip their locomotives with spark-arresters. They also are obliged to keep their rights of way free of material which burns readily. Spark-arresters are required also on logging engines.

The National and State Forests are posted with signs and notices asking the campers and tourists to be careful with campfires, tobacco and matches. Advertisements are run in newspapers, warning people to be careful so as not to set fire to the forests. Exhibits are made at fairs, shows, community meetings and similar gatherings, showing the dangers from forest fires and how these destructive conflagrations may be controlled. Every possible means is used to teach the public to respect and protect the forests.

For many years, the United States Forest Service and State Forestry Departments have been keeping a record of forest fires and their causes. Studies have been made of the length and character of each fire season. Information has been gathered concerning the parts of the forest where lightning is most likely to strike or where campfires are likely to be left by tourists. The spots or zones of greatest fire danger are located in this way and more forest guards are placed in these areas during the dangerous fire season. Careful surveys of this kind are aiding greatly in reducing the number of forest fires.

In trying to get all possible information about future weather conditions, the Forestry Departments cooeperate with the United States Weather Bureau. When the experts predict that long periods of dry weather or dangerous storms are approaching, the forest rangers are especially watchful, as during such times, the menace to the woods is greatest. The rangers also have big fire maps which they hang in their cabins. These maps show the location of dangerous fire areas, roads, trails, lookout-posts, cities, towns and ranches, sawmills, logging camps, telephone lines, fire tool boxes and other data of value to fire fighters. All this information is so arranged as to be readily available in time of need. It shows where emergency fire fighters, tools and food supplies can be secured, and how best to attack a fire in any certain district. A detailed plan for fighting forest fires is also prepared and kept on file at every ranger station.

The following are six rules which, if put in practice, will help prevent outbreaks of fires:

1. Matches. - Be sure your match is out. Break it in two before you throw it away.

2. Tobacco. - Throw pipe ashes and cigar or cigarette stubs in the dust of the road and stamp or pinch out the fire before leaving them. Don't throw them into the brush, leaves or needles.

3. Making camp. - Build a small campfire. Build it in the open, not against a tree or log, or near brush.

Scrape away the trash from all around it.

4. Leaving camp. - Never leave a campfire, even for a short time, without quenching it with water or earth. Be sure it is OUT.

5. Bonfires. - Never build bonfires in windy weather or where there is the slightest danger of their escaping from control. Don't make them larger than you need.

6. Fighting fires. - If you find a fire, try to put it out. If you can't, get word of it to the nearest United States forest ranger or State fire warden at once.

Remember "minutes count" in reporting forest fires.

Charles Lathrop Pack

CHAPTER VII

INSECTS AND DISEASES
THAT DESTROY FORESTS

Forest insects and tree diseases occasion heavy losses each year among the standing marketable trees. Insects cause a total loss of more than $100,000,000 annually to the forest products of the United States. A great number of destructive insects are constantly at work in the forests injuring or killing live trees or else attacking dead timber. Forest weevils kill tree seeds and destroy the young shoots on trees. Bark and timber beetles bore into and girdle trees and destroy the wood. Many borers and timber worms infest logs and lumber after they are cut and before they are removed from the forest. This scattered work of the insects here, there, and everywhere throughout the forests causes great damage.

Different kinds of flies and moths deposit their eggs on the leaves of the trees. After the eggs hatch, the baby caterpillars feed on the tender, juicy leaves. Some of the bugs destroy all the leaves and thus remove an important means which the tree has of getting food and drink. Wire worms attack the roots of the tree. Leaf hoppers suck on the sap supply of the leaves. Leaf rollers cause the leaves to curl up and die. Trees injured by fire fall easy prey before the attacks of forest insects. It takes a healthy, sturdy tree to escape injury by these pirates of the forests. There are more than five hundred insects that attack oak trees and at least two hundred and fifty different species that carry on destruction among the pines.

Insect pests have worked so actively that many forests have lost practically all their best trees of certain species. Quantities of the largest spruce trees in the Adirondacks have been killed off by bark beetles. The saw-fly worm has killed off most of the mature larches in these eastern forests. As they travel over the National and State Forests, the rangers are always on the watch for signs of tree infection. Whenever they notice red-brown masses of pitch and sawdust on the bark of the trees, they know that insects are busy there. Where the needles of a pine or spruce turn yellow or red, the presence of bark beetles is shown. Signs of pitch on the bark of coniferous trees are the first symptoms of infection. These beetles bore through the bark and into the wood. There they lay eggs. The parent beetles soon die but their children continue the work of burrowing in the wood. Finally, they kill the tree by making a complete cut around the trunk through the layers of wood that act as waiters to carry the food from the roots to the trunk, branches and leaves. The next spring these young develop into full-grown beetles, and come out from the diseased tree. They then attack new trees.

When the forest rangers find evidences of serious infection, they cut down the diseased trees. They strip the bark from the trunk and branches and burn it in the fall or winter when the beetles are working in the bark and can be destroyed most easily. If the infection of trees extends over a large tract, and there is a nearby market for the lumber the timber is sold as soon as possible. Trap trees are also used in controlling certain species of injurious forest insects. Certain trees are girdled with an ax so that they will become weakened or die, and thus provide easy means of entrance for the insects. The beetles swarm to such trees in great numbers. When the tree is full of insects, it is cut down and burned. In this way, infections which are not too severe can often be remedied.

The bark-boring beetles are the most destructive insects that attack our forests. They have wasted enormous tracts of pine timber throughout the southern states. The eastern spruce beetle has destroyed countless feet of spruce. The Engelmann spruce beetle has devastated many forests of the Rocky Mountains. The Black Hills beetle has killed billions of feet of marketable timber in the Black Hills of South Dakota. The hickory bark beetle, the Douglas fir beetle and the larch worm have been very destructive.

Forest fungi cause most of the forest tree diseases. A tree disease is any condition that prevents the tree from growing and developing in a normal, healthy manner. Acid fumes from smelters, frost, sunscald, dry or extremely wet weather, all limit the growth of trees. Leaf diseases lessen the food supplies of the trees. Bark diseases prevent the movement of the food supplies. Sapwood ailments cut off the water supply that rises from the roots. Seed and flower diseases prevent the trees from producing more of their kind.

Most of the tree parasites can gain entrance to the trees only through knots and wounds. Infection usually occurs through wounds in the tree trunk or branches caused by lightning, fire, or by men or animals. The cone-bearing trees give off pitch to cover such wounds. In this way they protect the injuries against disease infection. The hardwood trees are unable to protect their wounds as effectively as the evergreens. Where the wound is large, the exposed sapwood dies, dries out, and cracks. The fungi enter these cracks and work their way to the heartwood. Many of the fungi cannot live unless they reach the heartwood of the tree. Fires wound the base and trunks of forest trees severely so that they are exposed to serious destruction by heartrot.

Foresters try to locate and dispose of all the diseased trees in the State and Government forests. They strive to remove all the sources of tree disease from the woods. They can grow healthy trees if all disease germs are kept away from the timberlands. Some tree diseases have become established so strongly in forest regions that it is almost impossible to drive them out. For example, chestnut blight is a fungous disease that is killing many of our most valuable chestnut trees. The fungi of this disease worm their way through the holes in the bark of the trees, and spread around the trunk. Diseased patches or cankers form on the limbs or trunk of the tree. After the canker forms on the trunk, the tree soon dies. Chestnut blight has killed most of the chestnut trees in New York and Pennsylvania. It is now active in Virginia and West Virginia and is working its way down into North and South Carolina.

Diseased trees are a menace to the forest. They rob the healthy trees of space, light and food. That is why it is necessary to remove them as soon as they are discovered. In the smaller and older forests of Europe, tree surgery and doctoring are practiced widely. Wounds are treated and cured and the trees are pruned

Charles Lathrop Pack

and sprayed at regular intervals. In our extensive woods such practices are too expensive. All the foresters can do is to cut down the sick trees in order to save the ones that are sound.

There is a big difference between tree damages caused by forest insects and those caused by forest fungi and mistletoe. The insects are always present in the forest. However, it is only occasionally that they concentrate and work great injury and damage in any one section. At rare intervals, some very destructive insects may centre their work in one district. They will kill a large number of trees in a short time. They continue their destruction until some natural agency puts them to flight. The fungi, on the other hand, develop slowly and work over long periods. Sudden outbreaks of fungous diseases are unusual.

Heavy snows, lightning and wind storms also lay low many of the tree giants of the forest. Heavy falls of snow may weigh down the young, tall trees to such an extent that they break. Lightning - it is worst in the hills and mountains of the western states - may strike and damage a number of trees in the same vicinity. If these trees are not killed outright, they are usually damaged so badly that forest insects and fungi complete their destruction.

Big trees are sometimes uprooted during forest storms so that they fall on younger trees and cripple and deform them. Winds benefit the forests in that they blow down old trees that are no longer of much use and provide space for younger and healthier trees to grow. Usually the trees that are blown down have shallow roots or else are situated in marshy, wet spots so that their root-hold in the soil is not secure. Trees that have been exposed to fire are often weakened and blown down easily.

Where excessive livestock grazing is permitted in young forests considerable damage may result. Goats, cattle and sheep injure young seedlings by browsing. They eat the tender shoots of the trees. The trampling of sheep, especially on steep hills, damages the very young trees. On mountain sides the trampling of sheep frequently breaks up the forest floor of sponge-like grass and debris and thus aids freshets and floods. In the Alps of France sheep grazing destroyed the mountain forests and, later on, the grass which replaced the woods. Destructive floods resulted. It has cost the French people many millions of dollars to repair the damage done by the sheep.

The Federal Government does its best to keep foreign tree diseases out of the United States. As soon as any serious disease is discovered in foreign countries the Secretary of Agriculture puts in force a quarantine against that country. No seed or tree stock can be imported. Furthermore, all the new species of trees, cuttings or plants introduced to this country are given thorough examination and inspection by government experts at the ports where the products are received from abroad. All diseased trees are fumigated, or if found diseased, destroyed. In this manner the Government protects our country against new diseases which might come to our shores on foreign plants and tree stock.

CHAPTER VIII

THE GROWTH OF THE FORESTRY IDEA

Our forests of the New World were so abundant when the early settlers landed on the Atlantic Coast that it was almost impossible to find enough cleared land in one tract to make a 40-acre farm. These thick, dense timberlands extended westward to the prairie country. It was but natural, therefore, that the forest should be considered by these pioneers as an obstacle and viewed as an enemy. Farms and settlements had to be hewed out of the timberlands, and the forests seemed inexhaustible.

Experts say that the original, virgin forests of the United States covered approximately 822,000,000 acres. They are now shrunk to one-sixth of that area. At one time they were the richest forests in the world. Today there are millions of acres which contain neither timber nor young growth. Considerable can be restored if the essential measures are started on a national scale. Such measures would insure an adequate lumber supply for all time to come.

Rules and regulations concerning the cutting of lumber and the misuse of forests were suggested as early as the seventeenth century. Plymouth Colony in 1626 passed an ordinance prohibiting the cutting of timber from the Colony lands without official consent. This is said to be the first conservation law passed in America. William Penn was one of the early champions of the "Woodman, spare that tree" slogan. He ordered his colonists to leave one acre of forest for every five acres of land that were cleared.

In 1799 Congress set aside $200,000 for the purchase of a small forest reserve to be used as a supply source of ship timbers for the Navy. About twenty-five years later, it gave the President the power to call upon the Army and Navy whenever necessary to protect the live oak and red cedar timber so selected in Florida. In 1827, the Government started its first work in forestry. It was an attempt to raise live oak in the Southern States to provide ship timbers for the Navy. Forty years later, the Wisconsin State Legislature began to investigate the destruction of the forests of that state in order to protect them and prolong their life. Michigan and Maine, in turn, followed suit. These were some of the first steps taken to study our forests and protect them against possible extinction.

The purpose of the Timber Culture Act passed by Congress in 1873 was to increase national interest in reforestation. It provided that every settler who would plant and maintain 40 acres of timber in the treeless sections should be entitled to secure patent for 160 acres of the public domain - that vast territory consisting of all the states and territories west of the Mississippi, except Texas, as well as Ohio, Indiana, Illinois, Michigan, Wisconsin, Florida, Alabama and Mississippi. This act, as well as several State laws, failed because the settlers did not know enough about tree planting. The laws also were not effective because they did not prevent dishonest practices.

In 1876, the first special agent in forestry was appointed by the Commissioner of Agriculture to study the annual consumption, exportation and importation of timber and other forest products, the probable supply for future wants, and the means best adapted for forest preservation. Five years later, the Division of Forestry was organized as a branch of the Department of Agriculture. It was established in order to carry on investigations about forestry and how to preserve our trees.

For some nine years the Division of Forestry was nothing more than a department of information. It distributed technical facts and figures about the management of private woodlands and collected data concerning our forest resources. It did not manage any of the Government timberlands because there were no forest reserves at that time. It was not until 1891 that the first forest reserve, the Yellowstone Park Timberland Reserve, was created by special proclamation of President Harrison. Later it became part of the National Park reserves. Although the Division of Forestry had no special powers to oversee and direct the management of the forest reserves, during the next six years a total of 40,000,000 acres of valuable timberland were so designated and set aside. At the request of the Secretary of the Interior, the National Academy of Sciences therefore worked out a basis for laws governing national forests. Congress enacted this law in 1897. Thereafter the Department of the Interior had active charge of the timberlands. At that time little was known scientifically about the American forests. There were no schools of forestry in this country. During the period 1898-1903, several such schools were established.

President McKinley, during his term of office, increased the number of forest reserves from 28 to over 40, covering a total area of 30,000,000 acres. President Roosevelt added many millions of acres to the forest reserves, bringing the net total to more than 150,000,000 acres, including 159 different forests. In 1905, the administration of the forest reserves was transferred from the Department of the Interior to the Department of Agriculture, and their name changed to National Forests. No great additions to the government timberlands have been made since that time. Small, valuable areas have been added. Other undesirable tracts have been cut off from the original reserves.

The growth of the Division of Forestry, now the United States Forest Service, has been very remarkable since 1898, when it consisted of only a few scientific workers and clerks. At present it employs more than 2,600 workers, which number is increased during the dangerous fire season to from 4,000 to 5,000 employees. The annual appropriations have been increased from $28,500 to approximately $6,500,000. The annual income from Uncle Sam's woodlands is also on the gain and now amounts to about $5,000,000 yearly. This income results largely from the sale of timber and the grazing of livestock on the National Forests.

CHAPTER IX

OUR NATIONAL FORESTS

Our National Forests include 147 distinct and separate bodies of timber in twenty-seven different states and in Alaska and Porto Rico. They cover more than 156,000,000 acres. If they could be massed together in one huge area like the state of Texas, it would make easier the task of handling the forests and fighting fires. The United States Forest Service, which has charge of their management and protection, is one of the largest and most efficient organizations of its kind in the world. It employs expert foresters, scientists, rangers and clerks.

The business of running the forest is centred in eight district offices located in different parts of the country with a general headquarters at Washington, D.C. These districts are in charge of district foresters and their assistants.

The district headquarters and the States that they look after are:

No. 1.   Northern District, Missoula, Montana. (Montana, northeastern Washington, northern Idaho, and northwestern South Dakota.)

No. 2.   Rocky Mountain District, Denver, Colorado. (Colorado, Wyoming, the remainder of South Dakota, Nebraska, northern Michigan, and northern Minnesota.)

No. 3.   Southwestern District, Albuquerque, New Mexico. (Most of Arizona and New Mexico.)

No. 4.   Intermountain District, Ogden, Utah. (Utah, southern Idaho, western Wyoming, eastern and central Nevada, and northwestern Arizona.)

No. 5.   California District, San Francisco, California. (California and southwestern Nevada.)

No. 6.   North Pacific District, Portland, Oregon. (Washington and Oregon.)

No. 7.   Eastern District, Washington, D.C. (Arkansas, Alabama, Florida, Oklahoma, North Carolina, South Carolina, Georgia, Tennessee, Virginia, West Virginia, New Hampshire, Maine, and Porto Rico.)

No. 8.   Alaska District, Juneau, Alaska. (Alaska.)

Each of the National Forests is under the direct supervision of a forest supervisor and is split up into from 5 to 10 or more ranger districts. Each ranger district is in charge of a forest ranger who has an area of from 100,000 to 200,000 acres in his charge.

The National Forests are, for the most part, located in the mountainous region of the West, with small scattered areas in the Lake States, and the White Mountains, Southern Appalachians and Ozarks of the Eastern and Southern States. Many of them are a wilderness of dense timber. It is a huge task to protect these forests against the ravages of fire. Fire fighting takes precedence over all other work in the National Forests. Lookout stations are established on high points to watch for signs of fire. Airplanes are used on fire patrol over great areas of forest. Where railroads pass through the National Forests, rangers operate motor cars and hand-cars over the tracks in their patrol work. Launches are used in Alaska and on some of the forests where there are large lakes, to enable the fire fighters and forest guardians to cover their beats quickly. Every year the National Forests are being improved and made more accessible by the building of permanent roads, trails and telephone lines. Special trails are built to and in the fire protection areas of remote sections. A network of good roads is const- ructed in every forest to improve fire fighting activities as well as to afford better means of communication between towns, settlements and farms. The road and trail plan followed in the National Forests is mapped out years in advance. In the more remote sections, trails are first constructed. Later, these trails may be developed into wagon or motor roads. Congress annually appropriates large sums of money for the building of roads in the National Forests. Over 25,000 miles of roads and 35,000 miles of trails have already been constructed in these forests.

Communication throughout the National Forests is had by the use of the telephone and the radio or wireless telephone. Signalling by means of the heliograph is practiced on bright days in regions that have no telephones. Arrangements made with private telephone companies permit the forest officers to use their lines. The efficient communication systems aid in the administration of the forests and speeds the work of gathering fire fighters quickly at the points where smoke is detected.

Agricultural and forestry experts have surveyed the lands in the National Forests. Thus they have prevented the use of lands for forestry purposes which are better adapted for farming. Since 1910, more than 26,500,000 acres of lands have been excluded from the forests. These lands were more useful for farming or grazing than for forestry. Practically all lands within the National Forests have now been examined and classified. At intervals Congress has combined several areas of forest lands into single tracts. Government lands outside the National Forests have also been traded for state or private lands within their boundaries. Thus the forests have been lined-up in more compact bodies. Careful surveys are made before such trades are closed to make sure that the land given to Uncle Sam is valuable for timber production and the protection of stream flow, and that the Government receives full value for the land that is exchanged.

The National Forests contain nearly five hundred billion board feet of merchantable timber. This is 23 per cent. of the remaining timber in the country. Whenever the trees in the forest reach maturity they are sold and put to use. All green trees to be cut are selected by qualified forest officers and blazed and marked with a "U.S." This marking is done carefully so as to protect the forest and insure a future crop of trees on the area. Timber is furnished at low rates to local farmers, settlers, and stockmen for use in making improvements. Much fire wood and dead and down timber also is given away. The removal of such material lessens the fire danger in the forest.

Over a billion feet of timber, valued at more than $3,000,000, is sold annually from the National Forests.

One generally does not think of meat, leather and wool as forest crops. Nevertheless, the National Forests play an important part in the western livestock industry. Experts report that over one-fifth of the cattle and one-half of the sheep of the western states are grazed in the National Forests. These livestock are estimated to be worth nearly one-quarter billion dollars. More than 9,500,000 head of livestock are pastured annually under permit in the Federal forests. In addition, some 4,000,000 to 6,000,000 calves and lambs are grazed free of charge.

The ranges suitable for stock grazing are used to pasture sheep, cattle, horses, hogs and goats. The Secretary of Agriculture decides what number and what kind of animals shall graze on each forest. He regulates the grazing and prevents injury to the ranges from being overstocked with too many cattle and sheep. The forest ranges are divided into grazing units. Generally, the cattle and horses are grazed in the valleys and on the lower slopes of the mountain. The sheep and goats are pastured on the high mountain sides and in the grassy meadows at or above timberline.

Preferences to graze live stock on the forest ranges are for the most part granted to stockmen who own improved ranch property and live in or near one of the

National Forests. The fee for grazing on forest ranges is based on a yearlong rate of $1.20 a head of cattle, $1.50 for horses, $.90 for hogs and $.30 a head for sheep.

At times it is necessary, for short periods, to prohibit grazing on the Government forest ranges. For example, when mature timber has been cut from certain areas, it is essential that sheep be kept off such tracts until the young growth has made a good start in natural reforestation. Camping grounds needed for recreation purposes by the public are excluded from the grazing range. If a shortage of the water supply of a neighboring town or city threatens, or if floods or erosion become serious due to fire or overgrazing of the land, the range is closed to live-stock and allowed to recuperate. Where artificial planting is practiced, grazing is often forbidden until the young trees get a good start.

The total receipts which Uncle Sam collects from the 30,000 or more stockmen who graze their cattle and sheep on the National Forests amount to nearly $2,500,000 annually. As a result of the teachings of the Forest Service, the stockmen are now raising better livestock. Improved breeding animals are kept in the herds and flocks. Many of the fat stock now go directly from the range to the market. Formerly, most of the animals had to be fed on corn and grain in some of the Middle Western States to flesh them for market. Experiments have been carried on which have shown the advantages of new feeding and herding methods. The ranchers have banded together in livestock associations, which cooeeperate with the Forest Service in managing the forest ranges.

It costs about $5 to sow one acre of ground to tree seed, and approximately $10 an acre to set out seedling trees. The seed is obtained from the same locality where it is to be planted. In many instances, cones are purchased from settlers who make a business of gathering them. The Federal foresters dry these cones in the sun and thresh out the seed, which they then fan and clean. If it is desired to store supplies of tree seed from year to year it is kept in sacks or jars, in a cool, dry place, protected from rats and mice. Where seed is sown directly on the ground, poison bait must be scattered over the area in order to destroy the gophers, mice and chipmunks which otherwise would eat the seed. Sowing seed broadcast on unprepared land has usually failed unless the soil and weather conditions were just right. For the most part, setting out nursery seedlings has given better results than direct seeding. Two men can set out between five hundred and one thousand trees a day.

The National Forests contain about one million acres of denuded forest lands. Much of this was cut-over and so severely burned before the creation of the forests that it bears no tree growth. Some of these lands will reseed themselves naturally while other areas have to be seeded or planted by hand. In this way the lands that will produce profitable trees are fitted to support forest cover. Because the soils and climate of our National Forests are different, special experiments have been carried on in different places to decide the best practices to follow. Two method of reforestation are commonly practiced. In some places, the tree seed is sown directly upon the ground and, thereafter, may or may not be cultivated. This method is limited to the localities where the soil and moisture conditions are favorable for rapid growth. Under the other plan, the seedlings are grown in nurseries for several years under favorable conditions. They are then moved to the field and set out in permanent plantations.

CHAPTER X

THE NATIONAL FORESTS OF ALASKA

There are two great National Forests in Alaska. They cover 20,579,740 acres or about 5-1/2 per cent. of the total area of Alaska. The larger of these woodlands, the Tongass National Forest, is estimated to contain 70,000,000,000 board feet of timber ripe for marketing. Stands of 100,000 board feet per acre are not infrequent. This is the Alaskan forest that will some day be shipping large amounts of timber to the States. It has over 12,000 miles of shore line and ninety per cent. of the usable timber is within two miles of tidewater. This makes it easy to log the timber and load the lumber directly from the forests to the steamers. This forest is 1500 miles closer to the mainland markets than is the other Alaskan National Forest.

In most of the National Forests the rangers ride around their beats on horseback. The foresters in the Tongass use motor boats. They travel in couples; two men to a 35-foot boat, which is provided with comfortable eating and sleeping quarters. The rangers live on the boat all the time. During the summer they work sixteen to twenty hours daily. The days are long and the nights short, and they must travel long distances between points of work. On such runs one man steers the boat and watches the forested shoreline for three or four hours at a time, while his mate reads or sleeps; then they change off. In this way, they are able to make the most efficient use of the long periods of daylight.

The other big timberland in Alaska is the Chugach National Forest. It is a smaller edition of the Tongass Forest. Its trees are not so large and the stand of timber only about one-half as heavy as in the Tongass. Experts estimate that it contains 7,000,000,000 board feet of lumber. Western hemlock predominates. There is also much spruce, poplar and birch. Stands of 40,000 to 50,000 feet of lumber an acre are not unusual. In the future, the lumber of the Chugach National Forest will play an important part in the industrial life of Alaska. Even now, it is used by the fishing, mining, railroad and agricultural interests. On account of its great distance from the markets of the Pacific Northwest it will be a long time before lumber from this forest will be exported.

The timber in the Tongass National Forest runs 60 per cent. western hemlock and 20 per cent. Sitka spruce. The other 20 per cent. consists of western red cedar, yellow cypress, lodge-pole pine, cottonwood and white fir. The yellow cypress is very valuable for cabinet making. All these species except the cedar are suitable for pulp manufacture. Peculiarly enough, considerable of the lumber used in Alaska for box shooks in the canneries and in building work is imported from the United States. The local residents do not think their native timber is as good as that which they import.

Alaska will probably develop into one of the principal paper sources of the United States. Our National Forests in Alaska contain approximately 100,000,000 cords of timber suitable for paper manufacture. Experts report that these forests could produce 2,000,000 cords of pulpwood annually for centuries without depletion. About 6,000,000 tons of pulpwood annually are now required to keep us supplied with enough paper. The Tongass National Forest could easily supply one-third of this amount indefinitely. This forest is also rich in water power. It would take more than 250,000 horses to produce as much power as that which the streams and rivers of southern Alaska supply.

The western hemlock and Sitka spruce are the best for paper making. The spruce trees are generally sound and of good quality. The hemlock trees are not so good, being subject to decay at the butts. This often causes fluted trunks. The butt logs from such trees usually are inferior. This defect in the hemlock reduces its market value to about one-half that of the spruce for paper making. Some of the paper mills in British Columbia are now using these species of pulpwood and report that they make high-grade paper.

The pulp logs are floated down to the paper mill. In the mill the bark is removed from the logs. Special knives remove all the knots and cut the logs into pieces twelve inches long and six inches thick. These sticks then pass into a powerful grinding machine which tears them into small chips. The chips are cooked in special steamers until they are soft. The softened chips are beaten to pieces in large vats until they form a pasty pulp. The pulp is spread over an endless belt of woven wire cloth of small mesh. The water runs off and leaves a sheet of wet pulp which then is run between a large number of heated and polished steel cylinders which press and dry the pulp into sheets of paper. Finally, it is wound into large rolls ready for commercial use.

If a pulp and paper industry is built up in Alaska, it will be of great benefit to that northern country. It will increase the population by creating a demand for more labor. It will aid the farming operations by making a home market for their products. It will improve transportation and develop all kinds of business.

Altogether 420,000,000 feet of lumber have been cut and sold from the national forests of Alaska in the past ten years. This material has been made into such products as piling, saw logs and shingle bolts. All this lumber has been used in Alaska and none of it has been exported. Much of the timber was cut so that it would fall almost into tide-water. Then the logs were fastened together in rafts and towed to the sawmills. One typical raft of logs contained more than 1,500,000 feet of lumber. It is not unusual for spruce trees in Alaska to attain a diameter of from six to nine feet and to contain 10,000 or 15,000 feet of lumber.

Southeastern Alaska has many deep-water harbors which are open the year round. Practically all the timber in that section is controlled by the Government and is within the Tongass National Forest. This means that this important crop will be handled properly. No waste of material will occur. Cutting will be permitted only where the good of the forest justifies such work.

CHAPTER XI

PROGRESS IN STATE FORESTRY

The rapid depletion and threatened exhaustion of the timber supply in the more thickly populated sections of the East has prompted several of the states to initiate action looking toward the conservation of their timber resources. As far back as 1880, a forestry commission was appointed in New Hampshire to formulate a forest policy for the State. Vermont took similar action two years later, followed within the next few years by many of the northeastern and lake states.

These commissions were mainly boards of inquiry, for the purpose of gathering reliable information upon which to report, with recommendations, for the adoption of a state forest policy. As a result of the inquiries, forestry departments were established in a number of states. The report of the New York Commission of 1884 resulted in forest legislation, in 1885, creating a forestry department and providing for the acquisition of state forests. Liberal appropriations were made from time to time for this purpose, until now the state forests embrace nearly 2,000,000 acres, the largest of any single state.

New York state forests were created, especially, for the protection of the Adirondack and Catskill regions as great camping and hunting grounds, and not for timber production. The people of the state were so fearful that through political manipulation this vast forest resource might fall into the hands of the timber exploiters, that a constitutional amendment was proposed and adopted, absolutely prohibiting the cutting of green timber from the state lands. Thus, while New York owns large areas of state forest land, it is unproductive so far as furnishing timber supplies to the state is concerned. It is held distinctly for the recreation it affords to campers and hunters, and contains many famous summer resorts.

State forestry in Pennsylvania began in 1887, when a commission was appointed to study conditions, resulting in the establishment of a Commission of Forestry in 1895. Two years later, an act was passed providing for the purchase of state forests. At the present time, Pennsylvania has 1,250,000 acres of state forest land. Unlike those of New York, Pennsylvania forests were acquired and are managed primarily for timber production, although the recreational uses are not overlooked.

The large areas of state-owned lands in the Lake States suitable, mainly, for timber growing, enabled this section to create extensive state forests without the necessity of purchase as was the case in New York and Pennsylvania. As a result, Wisconsin has nearly 400,000 acres of state forest land, Minnesota, about 330,000, and Michigan, about 200,000 acres. South Dakota, with a relatively small area of forest land, has set aside 80,000 acres for state forest. A number of other states have initiated a policy of acquiring state forest lands, notably, New Hampshire, Vermont, Massachusetts, Connecticut, New Jersey, Maryland,

and Indiana, each with small areas, but likely to be greatly increased within the next few years under the development of present policies. Other states are falling in line with this forward movement. There are but 4,237,587 acres in state forests in the United States. This is only 1-1/2 per cent. of the cut-over and denuded land in the country which is useful only for tree production. The lack of funds prevents many states from embarking more extensively in this work. Many states set aside only a few thousand a year; others, that are more progressive and realize the need of forestry extension, spend annually from one hundred thousand to five hundred thousand dollars. Foresters are, generally, agreed that as much as 25 per cent. of the forest land of every state should be publicly owned for producing large sized timber, requiring seventy-five to one hundred years to grow, and which the private owner would not be interested in producing. National, state, or communal forests must supply it. All of these combined comprise a very small part of the forests of most of the states, so that much larger areas must be acquired by the states and the national government to safeguard our future timber supplies.

Not less than thirty-two states are actually engaged in state forestry work. Many of them have well-organized forestry departments, which, in states like New York and Pennsylvania, having large areas of state forests, are devoted largely to the care and protection of these lands. In other states having no state forests, the work is largely educational in character.

The most notable progress in forestry has been made in fire protection. All states having forestry departments lay especial emphasis upon forest protection, since it is recognized that only by protecting the forests from fire is it possible to succeed in growing timber crops. In fact, in most cases, the prevention of fire in itself is sufficient to insure re-growth and productive forests. Pennsylvania is spending $500,000 annually in protecting her forests from fire. The cooeperation of the Federal Government, under a provision of the Weeks Law which appropriates small sums of money for forest protection, provided the state will appropriate an equal or greater amount, has done much to encourage the establishment of systems of forest protection in many of the states.

The enormous areas of denuded, or waste land in the various states, comprising more than 80,000,000 acres, which can be made again productive only by forest planting, present another big problem in state forestry. Many of the states have established state forestry nurseries for the growing of tree seedlings to plant up these lands. The trees are either given away, or sold at cost, millions being distributed each year, indicating a live interest and growing sentiment in re-foresting waste lands.

The appalling waste of timber resources through excessive and reckless cutting, amounting to forest devastation, is deplorable, but we are helpless to prevent it. Since the bulk of woodlands are privately owned, and there are no effective laws limiting the cutting of timber with a view to conserving the supply, the only means of bringing about regulated cutting on private lands is through cooeperation with the owners. This is being done in some of the states in a limited way, through educational methods, involving investigations, reports, demonstrations, and other means of bringing improved forestry practices to the attention of existing owners and enlisting their cooeperation and support in forest conservation.

Forestry in the state, or in the nation, seems to progress no more rapidly than the timber disappears; in fact, the individual states do not take precaution to conserve their timber supplies until exhaustion is threatened. The damage has been largely done before the remedy is considered. We are today paying a tremendous toll for our lack of foresight in these matters. As a timber producing state becomes a timber importing state, (a condition existing in most of the eastern and middle states) we begin to pay a heavy toll in the loss of home industries dependent upon wood, and also in heavy freight charges on lumber that we must import from distant points to supply our needs. In many states, the expenditure of an amount for reforestation and fire protection equal to this freight bill on imported lumber would make the state self-supporting in a decade, instead of becoming worse off each year.

Marked progress has been made along the lines indicated, but few of the states have begun to measure up to their full responsibility in protecting their future timber supply.

CHAPTER XII

THE PLAYGROUNDS OF THE NATION

The public forests are steadily increasing in popularity as the playgrounds of the Nation. The woodlands offer splendid opportunities for camping, hunting, fishing and outdoor life. Millions of motorists now spend their vacations in the government and state forests. Railroads and automobiles make the forests accessible to all. Thousands of miles of improved motor highways lead into the very heart of the hills. More than 5,500,000 people annually visit the National Forests. Of this number, some 2,500,000 are campers, fishermen and hunters.

The forests provide cheap health insurance to all who will enjoy what they offer in sport and recreation. For example, over 1,000,000 vacationists visit Colorado's forests each year. If each person spent but five days in the forests, this would mean a total of 5,000,000 days or 50,000,000 hours of rest and enjoyment. Recreation at the beaches and amusement parks costs at least fifty cents an hour. Applying that rate to the free fun which the people get out of the forests, in Colorado in one year the tourists, campers and fishermen gained $25,000,000 worth of pleasure from the forests.

The National and State Forests furnish summer homes

for thousands of people who live in the neighboring cities and towns. Regular summer home sites are laid off in many of the forests. Usually these individual sites cover about one-quarter acre or less. They rent for $5 to $25 a year, depending on the location. A man can rent one of these camp grounds for a term of years. He can build a summer cottage or bungalow on it. There are no special rules about the size or cost of the houses. Uncle Sam requires only that the cottages be sightly and the surroundings be kept clean and sanitary. Many of the cabins are built for $150 to $300. Some of them are more permanent and cost from $3,000 to $5,000 or $10,000. In the Angeles National Forest in southern California, over sixteen hundred of these cottages are now in use and many more are being built.

Where there are dead or mature trees in the forest, near summer home sites, timber can be purchased at low prices for use in building cottages. Even the people of small means can build cabins in the forests and enjoy living in the mountains during the heat of the summer. These camps provide fine surroundings for the rompings and summer games of the children and young people.

In California a number of cities have set up municipal camps in the National Forests. At very low costs, the city residents can spend their vacations at these camps. Tents and cottages are provided. Facilities for all kinds of games and sports furnish recreation. Each family may stay at the camp for two weeks. The expenses are so low for meals and tents that the municipal camps furnish the best and cheapest vacation which the family of limited means can enjoy. These camps are very popular. Wherever they have been tried, they have been successful. There are twelve municipal camps in California. They cost $150,000.

Fine automobile camps are maintained along many of the important National and State Forest highways for the use of tourists. Concrete fireplaces, tables, benches and running water are provided at these wayside camping places. The tourists who carry their camp kits like to stop at these automobile camps. They meet many other tourists and exchange information about the best trails to follow and the condition of the roads. Sometimes, permanent cabins and shelters are provided for the use of the cross-country travelers. The only rules are that care be exercised in the use of fire and the camping sites be kept in clean and sanitary condition.

All the forest roads are posted with many signs asking the tourists to be careful in the use of matches, tobacco and camp fires, so as not to start destructive forest fires. In the Federal and State forests hundreds of man-caused fires occur annually, due to the neglect and carelessness of campers and tourists to put out their camp fires. A single match or a cigarette stub tossed from a passing automobile may start a costly fire. During the season from May to October, the western forests usually are as dry as tinder. Rains are rare during that period. A fire once started runs riot unless efficient control measures are used at once.

Those interested in fishing and hunting usually can find plenty of chance to pursue their favorite sports in the National and State Forests. There is good fishing in the forest streams and lakes, as the rangers, working in cooeperation with Federal and State hatcheries yearly restock important waters. Fishing and hunting in the National Forests are regulated by the fish and game laws of that state in which the forests are located. The killing of wild game is permitted during certain open seasons in most of the forest regions.

The eastern forests in the White Mountains, the Adirondacks, and the Appalachians, are not, for the most part, as well developed as recreation grounds as are the western vacation lands. However, more interest is being taken each year in the outdoor life features of the eastern forests, and ultimately they will be used on a large scale as summer camp grounds. Many hikers and campers now spend their annual vacations in these forests. Throughout the White Mountain forest of New Hampshire, regular trails for walking parties have been made. At frequent intervals simple camps for the use of travelers have been built by mountaineering clubs. This forest, located as it is near centres of large population is visited by a half-million tourists each season. The Pisgah National Forest of North Carolina is becoming a centre for automobile travel as it contains a fine macadam road. The Superior National Forest of Minnesota, which covers 1,250,000 acres and contains 150,000 acres of lakes, is becoming very popular. It is called "the land of ten thousand lakes." One can travel in a canoe through this forest for a month at a time without passing over the same lake twice. Other popular national forests are the Angeles in southern California, the Pike and Colorado in Colorado, and the Oregon and Wenatchee - the Pacific Northwest. Visitors to these forests total more than 1,750,000 a year.

The western forests are also being used for winter sports. They furnish excellent conditions for snow-shoe trips, skiing and sledding. The people who have camps on government land use their places for weekend excursions during the snow season when the roads are passable. The White Mountain National Forest is used more for winter sports than any other government woodland. At many of the towns of New Hampshire and Maine, huge carnivals are held each winter. Championship contests in skiing, snowshoeing, skating, ski jumping, tobogganing and ski-joring are held. Snow sport games are also annual events in the Routt, Leadville and Pike National Forests of Colorado. Cross country ski races and ski-joring contests are also held. In the Truckee National Forest of California, dog-team races over courses of 25 to 50 miles are held each winter.

About eighty per cent. of the 5,500,000 people who visit the National Forests are automobile tourists. The other twenty per cent. consists of sportsmen interested in hunting, fishing, canoeing, boating, mountain climbing, bathing, riding and hiking. In the Pacific Coast States there are a number of mountain climbing clubs whose members compete with each other in making difficult ascents. The mountaineering clubs of Portland, Oregon, for example, stage an interesting contest each summer in climbing Mount Hood, one of the highest peaks in the country.

CHAPTER XIII

SOLVING OUR FORESTRY PROBLEMS

A system of forestry which will provide sufficient lumber for the needs of our country and keep our forest land productive must be built on the extension of our public forests. Our National Forests are, at present, the one bright feature of future lumbering. Their tree crops will never be cut faster than they can be grown. A balance between production and consumption will always be maintained. Our needs for more timber, the necessity for protecting the headwaters of streams, the demands for saving wild life, and the playground possibilities of our forests justify their extension. Approximately eighty per cent of the American forests are now privately owned. The chances are that most of these wooded tracts will always remain in the hands of private owners. It is important that the production of these forests be kept up without injuring their future value. We must prepare for the lumber demands of many years from now.

Some method must be worked out of harnessing our idle forest lands and putting them to work growing timber. Any regulations that are imposed on the private owners of woodlands must be reasonable. Changes in our present methods of taxing timberlands must be made to encourage reforestation. The public must aid the private individuals in fighting forest fires, the greatest menace that modern forestry has to face. A national policy is needed which will permit the private owner to grow trees which will give him fair and reasonable profit when sold.

The farmers of this country use about one-half of all the lumber consumed annually. They own approximately 191,000,000 acres of timber in their farm woodlots. If farmers would devote a little time and labor to the permanent upkeep and improvement of their timber, they would aid in decreasing the danger of a future lumber famine. If they would but keep track of the acreage production of their woodlands as closely as they do of their corn and wheat crops, American forestry would benefit greatly.

Between 1908 and 1913, the U.S. Forest Service established two forest experiment stations in California and one each in Washington, Idaho, Colorado, and Arizona. They devote the same degree of science and skill to the solution of tree growing and lumbering problems as the agricultural experiment stations give to questions of farm and crop management. Despite the fact that these forestry stations did fine work for the sections that they served, recently a number of them had to close, due to lack of funds. Congress does not yet realize the importance of this work.

More forest experiment stations are needed throughout the country. Such problems as what kinds of trees are best to grow, must be solved. Of the 495 species of trees in this country, 125 are important commercially. They all differ in their histories, characteristics and requirements. Research and study should be made of these trees in the sections where they grow best. Our knowledge regarding tree planting and the peculiarities of the different species is, as yet, very meagre. We must discover the best methods of cutting trees and of disposing of the slash. We must investigate rates of growth, yields and other problems of forest management. We must study the effect of climate on forest fires. We must continue experiments in order to develop better systems of fire protection.

We need more forest experiment stations to promote the production of more timber. Twenty of our leading industries utilize lumber as their most important raw material. Fifty-five different industries use specialized grades and quality of lumber in the manufacture of many products. This use of lumber includes general mill work and planing mill products, such as building crates and boxes, vehicles, railroad cars, furniture, agricultural implements and wooden ware.

Our manufacturers make and use more than two hundred and seventy-five different kinds of paper, including newsprint, boxboard, building papers, book papers and many kinds of specialty papers. The forest experiment stations would help solve the practical problems of these many industries. They could work out methods by which to maintain our forests and still turn out the thirty-five to forty billion board feet of lumber used each year. They are needed to determine methods of increasing our annual cut for pulp and paper. They are necessary so that we can increase our annual output of poles, pilings, cooperage and veneer.

A forest experiment station is needed in the southern pine belt. The large pine forests of Dixieland have been shaved down from 130,000,000 acres to 23,500,000 acres. In that region there are more than

30,000,000 acres of waste forest lands which should be reclaimed and devoted to the growing of trees. Eastern and middle western manufacturing and lumbering centres are interested in the restoring of the southern pine forests. During the last score of years, they have used two-thirds of the annual output of those forests. In another ten to fifteen years home demand will use most of the pine cut in the South. The East and Middle West will then have to rely mostly on the Pacific Coast forests for their pine lumber.

The Lake States need a forest experiment station to work out methods by which the white pine, hemlock, spruce, beech, birch and maple forests of that section can be renewed. The Lake States are now producing only one-ninth as much white pine as they were thirty years ago. These states now cut only 3,500,000,000 feet of all kinds of lumber annually. Their output is growing smaller each year. Wisconsin led the United States in lumber production in 1900. Now she cuts less than the second-growth yield of Maine. Michigan, which led in lumber production before Wisconsin, now harvests a crop of white pine that is 50 per cent. smaller than that of Massachusetts. Experts believe that a forest experiment station in the Lake States would stimulate production so that enough lumber could be produced to satisfy the local demands.

Not least in importance among the forest regions requiring an experiment station are the New England States and northern and eastern New York. In that section there are approximately 25,000,000 acres of forest lands. Five and one-half million acres consist of waste and idle land. Eight million acres grow nothing but fuel-wood. The rest of the timber tracts are not producing anywhere near their capacity. New England produces 30 per cent. and New York 50 per cent. of our newsprint. Maine is the leading state in pulp production. New England imports 50 per cent. of her lumber, while New York cuts less than one-half the timber she annually consumes.

Another experiment station should be provided to study the forestry problems of Pennsylvania, southern and western New York, Ohio, Maryland, New Jersey and Delaware. At one time this region was the most important lumber centre of the United States. Pennsylvania spends $100,000,000 a year in importing lumber which should be grown at home. The denuded and waste lands at the headwaters of the Allegheny River now extend over one-half million acres. New Jersey is using more than twenty times as much lumber as is produced in the state. Ohio is a centre for wood manufacturing industries, yet her timber-producing possibilities are neglected, as are those of other states needing wood for similar purposes.

European nations have spent large sums of money in investigating forestry problems to make timber producing economically feasible, and have found that it paid. In this country, our forest experiment stations will have to deal with a timbered area twice that of all Europe, exclusive of Russia. That is why we shall need many of these stations to help solve the many questions of national welfare which are so dependent upon our forests.

CHAPTER XIV

WHY THE UNITED STATES SHOULD PRACTICE FORESTRY

Of late years the demand for lumber by the world trade has been very great. Most of the countries which have extensive forests are taking steps to protect their supplies. They limit cutting and restrict exports of timber. Both New Zealand and Switzerland have passed laws of this kind. Sweden exports much lumber, but by law forbids the cutting of timber in excess of the annual growth. Norway regulates private cutting. England is planning to plant 1,770,000 acres of new forest reserve. This body of timber when ready for cutting, would be sufficient to supply her home needs in time of emergency for at least three years. France is enlarging her forest nurseries and protecting her timber in every possible way. Even Russia, a country with huge forest tracts, is beginning to practice conservation. Russia now requires that all timber cut under concession shall be replaced by plantings of trees.

For many years, the United States and China were the greatest wasters of forest resources under the sun. Now this country has begun to practice scientific forestry on a large scale so that China now has the worst-managed forests in the world. Japan, on the other hand, handles her forests efficiently and has established a national forestry school. Austria, Norway, Sweden and Italy have devoted much time, labor and money to the development of practical systems of forestry. Turkey, Greece, Spain and Portugal, all follow sane and sensible forestry practices. Even Russia takes care of her national timberlands and annually draws enormous incomes from their maintenance. France and Germany both have highly successful forestry systems. Switzerland, Australia, and New Zealand are using their forests in a practical manner and saving sufficient supplies of wood for posterity.

History tells us that the forests first were protected as the homes of wild game. Little attention was paid to the trees in those days. The forests were places to hunt and abodes devoted to wild animals. Scientific forestry was first studied and practised widely in the nineteenth century. Its development and expansion have been rapid. Germany still leads as one of the most prominent countries that practices efficient forestry. German forests are now said to be worth more than $5,000,000,000. France has over 2,750,000 acres of fine publicly owned forests, in addition to private forests, which yield a net income of more than $2 an acre a year to the government. The French have led in extending reforestation on denuded mountain sides. British India has well-managed forests which cover over 200,000 square miles of area. These timberlands return a net income of from $3,000,000 to $4,000,000 a year. India now protects more than 35,000 square miles of forest against fire at an annual cost of less than half a cent an acre.

Forest experts say that the United States, which produces more than one-half of all the sawed timber in the world, should pay more attention to the export lumber business. Such trade must be built up on the basis of a permanent supply of timber. This means the practice of careful conservation and the replacement of forests that have been destroyed. We can not export timber from such meagre reserves as the pine forests of the South, which will not supply even the domestic needs of the region for much more than ten or fifteen years longer. Many of our timber men desire to develop extensive export trade. Our sawmills are large enough and numerous enough to cut much more timber annually than we need in this country. However, the danger is that we shall only abuse our forests the more and further deplete the timber reserves of future generations as a result of extensive export trade. If such trade is developed on a large scale, a conservative, practical national forestry policy must be worked out, endorsed and lived up to by every producing exporter.

The U.S. Forest Service reports that before the world war, we were exporting annually 3,000,000,000 board feet of lumber and sawlogs, not including ties, staves and similar material. This material consisted of Southern yellow pine, Douglas fir, white oak, redwood, white pine, yellow poplar, cypress, walnut, hickory, ash, basswood and similar kinds of wood. The exports were made up of 79 per cent. softwoods and 21 per cent. hardwoods. The export trade consumed about 8-1/2 per cent. of our annual lumber cut. Southern yellow pine was the most popular timber shipped abroad. One-half of the total export was of this material.

During the four years before the war our imports of lumber from foreign countries amounted to about 1,200,000,000 board feet of lumber and logs. In 1918,

imports exceeded exports by 100,000,000 board feet. In addition to this lumber, we also shipped in, largely from Canada, 1,370,000 cords of pulp wood, 596,000 tons of wood pulp, 516,000 tons of paper, and close to a billion shingles. Some of the material, such as wood pulp and paper, also came from Sweden, Norway, Germany, Spain, the Netherlands and the United Kingdom.

As a result of the war, European countries for several years can use 7,000,000,000 feet of lumber a year above their normal requirements. For housing construction, England needs 2,000,000,000 feet a year more than normally; France, 1,500,000,000 feet; Italy, 1,750,000,000 feet; Belgium and Spain 750,000,000 feet apiece. Even before the war, there was a great deficiency of timber in parts of Europe. It amounted to 16,000,000,000 board feet a year and was supplied by Russia, the United States, Canada, Sweden, Austria-Hungary and a few other countries of western Europe. If we can regulate cutting and replenish our forests as they deserve, there is a remarkable opportunity for us to build up a large and permanent export trade.

The Central and South American countries now have to depend on Canada, the United States and Sweden for most of their softwoods. Unless they develop home forests by the practice of modern forestry, they will always be dependent on imported timber of this type. South Africa and Egypt are both heavy importers of lumber. Africa has large tropical forests but the timber is hard to get at and move. China produces but little lumber and needs much. She is developing into a heavy importing country. Japan grows only about enough timber to supply her home needs. Australia imports softwoods from the United States and Canada.

New Zealand is in the market for Douglas fir and hardwoods.

In the past, our export lumber business has been second only to that of Russia in total amount. The value of the timber that we exported was larger than that of Russia because much of our timber that was sent abroad consisted of the best grades of material grown in this country. In the future, we shall have to compete in the softwood export business with Russia, Finland, Sweden, Norway and the various states of southeastern Europe which sell lumber. In the hardwood business, we have only a limited number of rivals. With the exception of a small section of eastern Europe, our hardwood forests are the finest in the Temperate Zone. We export hickory, black walnut, yellow poplar, white and red oak even to Russia and Sweden, countries that are our keenest rivals in the softwood export business.

Europe wants export lumber from our eastern states because the transportation costs on such material are low. She does not like to pay heavy costs of hauling timber from the Pacific Coast to the Atlantic seaboard and then have it reshipped by water.

Our eastern forests are practically exhausted. Our supplies of export lumber except Douglas fir are declining. Most of the kinds of export timber that Europe wants we need right at home. We have only about 258,000,000,000 feet of southern yellow pine left, yet this material composes one-half of our annual shipments abroad. We are cutting this material at the rate of 16,000,000,000 board feet a year. Some authorities believe that our reserves will last only sixteen years unless measures to protect them are put into effect at once. At the present rate of cutting long-leaf pine trees, our outputs of naval stores including turpentine and rosin are dwindling. We cannot afford to increase our export of southern yellow pine unless reforestation is started on all land suitable for that purpose. Our pine lands of the southern states must be restocked and made permanently productive. Then they could maintain the turpentine industry, provide all the lumber of this kind we need for home use, and supply a larger surplus for export.

Although our supplies of Douglas fir, western white pine, sugar pine and western yellow pine are still large, they will have to bear an extra burden when all the southern pine is gone. This indicates that the large supplies of these woods will not last as long as we would wish. To prevent overtaxing their production, it is essential that part of the load be passed to the southern pine cut-over lands. By proper protection and renewal of our forests, we can increase our production of lumber and still have a permanent supply. The Forest Service estimates that by protecting our cut-over and waste lands from fire and practicing care to secure reproduction after logging on our remaining virgin forest land, we can produce annually at least 27,750,000,000 cubic feet of wood, including 70,000,000,000 board feet of sawtimber. Such a production would meet indefinitely the needs of our growing population, and still leave an amount of timber available for export.

Our hardwoods need protection as well as our softwoods. Ten per cent of our yearly cut of valuable white oak is shipped overseas. In addition we annually waste much of our best oak in the preparation of split staves for export. At the present rate of cutting, the supply, it is said, will not last more than twenty-five years. We ship abroad about seven per cent. of our poplar lumber. Our supplies of this material will be exhausted in about twenty years if the present rate of cutting continues. We sell to foreign countries at least one-half of our cut of black walnut which will be exhausted in ten to twelve years unless present methods are reformed. Our supplies of hickory, ash and basswood will be used up in twenty to thirty years. We need all this hardwood lumber for future domestic purposes. However, the furniture factories of France, Spain and Italy are behind on orders. They need hardwood and much of our valuable hardwood timber is being shipped to Europe.

Experience has proved that correct systems of handling the private forests can not be secured by mere suggestions or education. No ordinary method of public cooeperation has been worked out which produces the desired results. It is necessary that suitable measures be adopted to induce private owners to preserve and protect their woodlands. The timber-lands must be protected against forest fires. Timber must be cut so as to aid natural reproduction of forest. Cut-over lands must be reforested. If such methods were practiced, and national, state and municipal forests were established and extended, our lumber problem would largely solve itself. We not only should produce a large permanent supply of timber for domestic use, but also should have great reserves available for export. Under such conditions, the United States would become the greatest supply source in the world for lumber.

CHAPTER XV

WHY THE LUMBERMAN SHOULD PRACTICE FORESTRY

The lumber industry of this country can aid reforestation by practicing better methods. It can harvest its annual crop of timber without injuring the future production of the forests. It can limit forest fires by leaving the woods in a safe condition after it has removed the timber. Some private timber owners who make a living out of cutting lumber, have even reached the stage where they are planting trees. They are coming to appreciate the need for replacing trees that they cut down, in order that new growth may develop to furnish future timber crops.

The trouble in this country has been that the lumbermen have harvested the crop of the forests in the shortest possible time instead of spreading out the work over a long period. Most of our privately owned forests have been temporarily ruined by practices of this sort. The aim of the ordinary lumberman is to fell the trees and reduce them to lumber with the least labor possible. He does not exercise special care as to how the tree is cut down. He pays little attention to the protection of young trees and new growth. He cuts the tree to fall in the direction that best serves his purpose, no matter whether this means that the forest giant will crush and seriously cripple many young trees. He wastes large parts of the trunk in cutting. He leaves the tops and chips and branches scattered over the ground to dry out. They develop into a fire trap.

As generally followed, the ordinary method of lumbering is destructive of the forests. It ravages the future production of the timberlands. It pays no heed to the young growth of the forest. It does not provide for the proper growth and development of the future forest. Our vast stretches of desolate and deserted cut-over lands are silent witnesses to the ruin which has been worked by the practice of destructive lumbering. Fortunately, a change for the better is now developing. With the last of our timberland riches in sight on the Pacific Coast, the lumbering industry is coming to see that it must prepare for the future. Consequently, operators are handling the woods better than ever before. They now are trying to increase both the production and permanent value of the remaining forests. They aim to harvest the tree yield more thoroughly and to extend their cuttings over many years. They appreciate that it is necessary to protect and preserve the forest at the same time that profitable tree crops are being removed. They see the need for saving and increasing young growth and for protecting the woodlands against fire. If only these methods of forestry had been observed from the time the early settlers felled the first trees, not only would our forests be producing at present all the lumber we could use, but also the United States would be the greatest lumber-exporting country in the world.

It will never be possible to stop timber cutting entirely in this country, nor would it be desirable to do so. The demands for building material, fuel, wood pulp and the like are too great to permit of such a condition. The Nation would suffer if all forest cutting was suspended. There is a vital need, however, of perpetuating our remaining forests. Wasteful lumbering practices should be stopped. Only trees that are ready for harvest should be felled. They should be cut under conditions which will protect the best interests and production of the timberlands. As a class, our lumbermen are no more selfish or greedy than men in many other branches of business. They have worked under peculiar conditions in the United States. Our population was small as compared with our vast forest resources. Conditions imposed in France and Germany, where the population is so dense that more conservative systems of lumbering are generally practiced, were not always applicable in this country. Furthermore, our lumbermen have known little about scientific forestry. This science is comparatively new in America. All our forestry schools are still in the early stages of their development. As lumbermen learn more about the value of modern forestry they gradually are coming to practice its principles.

The early lumbermen often made mistakes in estimating the timber yields of the forests. They also neglected to provide for the future production of the woodlands after the virgin timber was removed. Those who followed in their steps have learned by these errors what mistakes to avoid. Our lumbermen lead the world in skill and ingenuity. They have worked out most efficient methods of felling and logging the trees. Many foreign countries have long practiced forestry and lumbering, yet their lumbermen cannot compete with the Americans when it comes to a matter of ingenuity in the woods. American woods and methods of logging are peculiar. They would no more fit under

European forest conditions than would foreign systems be suitable in this country. American lumbermen are slowly coming to devise and follow a combination method which includes all the good points of foreign forestry revised to apply to our conditions.

We can keep our remaining forests alive and piece out their production over a long period if we practice conservation methods generally throughout the country. Our remaining forests can be lumbered according to the rules of practical forestry without great expense to the owners. In the long run, they will realize much larger returns from handling the woods in this way. This work of saving the forests should begin at once. It should be practiced in every state. Our cut-over and idle lands should be put to work. Our forest lands should be handled just like fertile farming lands that produce big crops. The farmer does not attempt to take all the fertility out of the land in the harvest of one bumper crop. He handles the field so that it will produce profitable crops every season. He fertilizes the soil and tills it so as to add to its productive power. Similarly, our forests should be worked so that they will yield successive crops of lumber year after year.

Lumbermen who own forests from which they desire to harvest a timber crop should first of all survey the woods, or have some experienced forester do this work, to decide on what trees should be cut and the best methods of logging to follow. The trees to be cut should be selected carefully and marked. The owner should determine how best to protect the young and standing timber during lumbering. He should decide on what plantings he will make to replace the trees that are cut. He should survey and estimate the future yield of the forest. He should study the young trees and decide about when they will be ripe to cut and what they will yield. From this information, he can determine his future income from the forest and the best ways of handling the woodlands.

Under present conditions in this country, only those trees should be cut from our forests which are mature and ready for the ax. This means that the harvest must be made under conditions where there are enough young trees to take the place of the full-grown trees that are removed. Cutting is best done during the winter when the trees are dormant. If the cutting is performed during the spring or summer, the bark, twigs and leaves of the surrounding young growth may be seriously damaged by the falling trees. The trees should be cut as low to the ground as is practicable, as high stumps waste valuable timber. Care should be taken so that they will not break or split in falling. Trees should be dropped so that they will not crush young seedlings and sapling growth as they fall. It is no more difficult or costly to throw a tree so that it will not injure young trees than it is to drop it anywhere without regard for the future of the forest.

Directly after cutting, the fallen timber should be trimmed so as to remove branches that are crushing down any young growth or seedling. In some forests the young growth is so thick that it is impossible to throw trees without falling them on some of these baby trees which will spring back into place again if the heavy branches are removed at once. The top of the tree should be trimmed so that it will lie close to the ground. Under such conditions it will rot rapidly and be less of a fire menace. The dry tops of trees which lodge above the ground are most dangerous sources of fire as they burn easily and rapidly.

The lumbermen can also aid the future development of the forests by using care in skidding and hauling the logs to the yard or mill. Care should be exercised in the logging operations not to tear or damage the bark of trunks of standing timber. If possible, only the trees of unimportant timber species should be cut for making corduroy roads in the forests. This will be a saving of valuable material.

In lumbering operations as practiced in this country, the logs are usually moved to the sawmills on sleds or by means of logging railroads. If streams are near by, the logs are run into the water and floated to the mill. If the current is not swift enough, special dams are built. Then when enough logs are gathered for the drive, the dam is opened and the captive waters flood away rapidly and carry the logs to the mill. On larger streams and rivers, the logs are often fastened together in rafts. Expert log drivers who ride on the tipping, rolling logs in the raging river, guide the logs on these drives.

On arrival at the sawmill, the logs are reduced to lumber. Many different kinds of saws are used in this work. One of the most efficient is the circular saw which performs rapid work. It is so wide in bite, however, that it wastes much wood in sawdust. For example, in cutting four boards of one-inch lumber, an ordinary circular saw wastes enough material to make a fifth board, because it cuts an opening that is one-quarter of an inch in width. Band saws, although they do not work at such high speed, are replacing circular saws in many mills because they are less wasteful of lumber. Although sawmills try to prevent waste of wood by converting slabs and short pieces into laths and shingles, large amounts of refuse, such as sawdust, slabs and edgings, are burned each season. As a rule, only about one-third of the tree is finally used for construction purposes, the balance being wasted in one way or another.

CHAPTER XVI

WHY THE FARMER SHOULD PRACTICE FORESTRY

The tree crop is a profitable crop for the average farmer to grow. Notwithstanding the comparatively sure and easy incomes which result from the farm woodlands that are well managed, farmers as a class neglect their timber. Not infrequently they sell their timber on the stump at low rates through ignorance of the real market value of the wood. In other cases, they do not care for their woodlands properly. They cut without regard to future growth. They do not pile the slashings and hence expose the timber tracts to fire dangers. They convert young trees into hewed crossties which would yield twice as great a return if allowed to grow for four or five years longer and then be cut as lumber.

Just to show how a small tract of trees will grow into money if allowed to mature, the case of a three-acre side-hill pasture in New England is interesting. Forty-four years ago the farmer who owned this waste land dug up fourteen hundred seedling pines which were growing in a clump and set them out on the sidehill. Twenty years later the farmer died. His widow sold the three acres of young pine for $300. Fifteen years later the woodlot again changed hands for a consideration of

$1,000, a lumber company buying it. Today, this small body of pine woods contains 90,000 board feet of lumber worth at least $1,500 on the stump. The farmer who set out the trees devoted about $35 worth of land and labor to the miniature forest. Within a generation this expenditure has grown into a valuable asset which yielded a return of $34.09 a year on the investment.

A New York farmer who plays square with his woodland realizes a continuous profit of $1 a day from a 115-acre timber tract. The annual growth of this well-managed farm forest is .65 cords of wood per acre, equivalent to 75 cords of wood - mostly tulip poplar - a year. The farmer's profit amounts to $4.68 a cord, or a total of $364.50 from the entire timber tract. Over in New Hampshire, an associate sold a two-acre stand of white pine - this was before the inflated war prices were in force - for $2,000 on the stump. The total cut of this farm forest amounted to 254 cords equivalent to 170,000 board feet of lumber. This was an average of about 85,000 feet an acre. The trees were between eighty and eighty-five years old when felled. This indicates an annual growth on each acre of about 1,000 feet of lumber. The gross returns from the sale of the woodland crops amounted to $12.20 an acre a year. These, of course, are not average instances.

Farmers should prize their woodlands because they provide building material for fences and farm outbuildings as well as for general repairs. The farm woodland also supplies fuel for the farm house. Any surplus materials can be sold in the form of standing timber, sawlogs, posts, poles, crossties, pulpwood, blocks or bolts. The farm forest also serves as a good windbreak for the farm buildings. It supplies shelter for the livestock during stormy weather and protects the soil against erosion. During slack times, it provides profitable work for the farm hands.

There are approximately one-fifth of a billion acres of farm woodlands in the United States. In the eastern United States there are about 169,000,000 acres of farmland forests. If these woodlands could be joined together in a solid strip one hundred miles wide, they would reach from New York to San Francisco. They would amount to an area almost eight times as large as the combined forests of France which furnished the bulk of the timber used by the Allies during the World War.

In the North, the farm woodlands compose two-fifths of all the forests. Altogether there are approximately 53,000,000 acres of farm woodlots which yield a gross income of about $162,000,000 annually to their owners. Surveys show that in the New England States more than 65 per cent. of the forested land is on farms, while in Ohio, Indiana, Illinois and Iowa from 80 to 100 per cent. of the timber tracts are on corn belt farms. Conditions in the South also emphasize the importance of farm woods, as in this region there are more than 125,000,000 acres which yield an income of about $150,000,000 a year. In fact the woodlands on the farms compose about 50 per cent. of all the forest lands south of the Mason-Dixon line. In Maryland, Virginia, North Carolina, Kentucky and Oklahoma, over 60 per cent. of all the forest land is on farms.

The Government says timber raising is very profitable in the Eastern States because there is plenty of cheap land which is not suitable for farming, while the rainfall is abundant and favors rapid tree growth. Furthermore, there are many large cities which use enormous supplies of lumber. The transportation facilities, both rail and water, are excellent. This section is a long distance from the last of the virgin forests of the Pacific Coast country.

The farms that reported at the last census sold an average of about $82 worth of tree crop products a year. New York, North Carolina, Virginia, Georgia, Tennessee, Alabama, Kentucky, Wisconsin and Pennsylvania each sold over $15,000,000 worth of lumber and other forest products from their farm woodlots during a single season. In 1918 the report showed that the farms of the country burn up about 78,000,000 cords of firewood annually, equal to approximately 11.5 cords of fuel a farm. The Southern States burn more wood than the colder Northern States. In North Carolina each farm consumes eighteen cords of fuel annually, while the farms of South Carolina and Arkansas used seventeen cords apiece, and those of Mississippi, Georgia, Tennessee, Louisiana, and Kentucky from fifteen to sixteen cords. Even under these conditions of extensive cordwood use, our farm woodlots are producing only about one-third to one-half of the wood supplies which they could grow if they were properly managed.

The farmer who appreciates the importance of caring for his home forests is always interested in knowing how much timber will grow on an acre during a period of twelve months. The Government reports that where the farm woodlots are fully stocked with trees and well-cared for, an acre of hardwoods will produce from one-half to one cord of wood - a cord of wood is equal to about 500 board feet of lumber. A pine forest will produce from one to two cords of wood an acre. The growth is greater in the warmer southern climate than it is in the North where the growing season is much shorter. Expert foresters say that posts and crossties can be grown in from ten to thirty years and that most of the rapid growing trees will make saw timber in between twenty and forty years.

After the farm woodland is logged, a new stand of young trees will develop from seeds or sprouts from the stumps. Farmers find that it is profitable to harrow the ground in the cut-over woodlands to aid natural reproduction, or to turn hogs into the timber tract to rustle a living as these animals aid in scattering the seed under favorable circumstances. It is also note-worthy that the most vigorous sprouts come from the clean, well-cut stumps from which the trees were cut during the late fall, winter or early spring before the sap begins to flow. The top of each stump should be cut slanting so that it will readily shed water. The trees that reproduce by sprouts include the oak, hickory, basswood, chestnut, gum, cottonwood, willows and young short-leaf and pitch pines.

In order that the farm woodland may be kept in the best of productive condition, the farmer should remove for firewood the trees adapted only for that purpose. Usually, removing these trees improves the growth of the remaining trees by giving them better chances to develop. Trees should be cut whose growth has been stunted because trees of more rapid growth crowded them out. Diseased trees or those that have been seriously injured by insects should be felled. In sections exposed to chestnut blight or gypsy moth infection, it is advisable to remove the chestnut and birch trees before they are damaged seriously. It is wise management to cut the fire-scarred trees as well as those that are crooked, large-crowned and shortboled, as they will not make good lumber. The removal of these undesirable trees improves the forest by providing more growing space for the sturdy, healthy trees. Sound dead trees as well as the slow-growing trees that crowd the fast growing varieties should be cut. In addition, where such less valuable trees as the beech, birch, black oak, jack oak or black gum are crowding valuable trees like the sugar maples, white or short-leaf pines, yellow poplar or white oak, the former species should be chopped down. These cutting operations should be done with the least possible damage to the living and young trees. The "weed trees" should be cut down, just as the weeds are hoed out of a field of corn, in order that the surviving trees may make better growth.

Often the farmer errs in marketing his tree crops. There have been numerous instances where farmers have been deluded by timber cruisers and others who purchased their valuable forest tracts for a mere fraction of what the woodlands were really worth. The United States Forest Service and State Forestry Departments have investigated many of these cases and its experts advise farmers who are planning to sell tree crops to get prices for the various wood products from as many sawmills and wood-using plants as possible. The foresters recommend that the farmers consult with their neighbors who have sold timber. Sometimes it may pay to sell the timber locally if the prices are right, as then the heavy transportation costs are eliminated. Most states have state foresters who examine woodlands and advise the owner just what to do. It pays to advertise in the newspapers and secure as many competitive bids as possible for the timber on the stump. Generally, unless the prices offered for such timber are unusually high, the farmer will get greater returns by logging and sawing the timber and selling it in the form of lumber and other wood products. The farmer who owns a large forest tract should have some reliable and experienced timberman carefully inspect his timber and estimate the amount and value. The owner should deal with only responsible buyers. He should use a written agreement in selling timber, particularly where the purchaser is to do the cutting. The farm woodland owner must always bear in mind that standing timber can always be held over a period of low prices without rapid deterioration. In selling lumber, the best plan is to use the inferior timber at home for building and repair work and to market the best of the material.

CHAPTER XVII

PUTTING WOOD WASTE TO WORK

For many years technical studies of wood were neglected. Detailed investigations of steel, concrete, oil, rubber and other materials were made but wood apparently was forgotten. It has been only during the last decade since the establishment of the Forest Products Laboratory of the United States Forest Service, at Madison, Wisconsin, that tests and experiments to determine the real value of different woods have been begun. One of the big problems of the government scientists at that station, which is conducted in cooeperation with the University of Wisconsin, is to check the needless waste of wood. By actual test they find out all about the wasteful practices of lumbering in the woods and mills. Then they try to educate and convert the lumbermen and manufacturers away from such practices.

The laboratory experts have already performed more than 500,000 tests with 149 different kinds of native woods. As a result of these experiments, these woods are now being used to better advantage with less waste in the building and manufacturing industries. A potential saving of at least 20 per cent. of the timbers used for building purposes is promised, which means a salvage of about $40,000,000 annually as a result of strength tests of southern yellow pine and Douglas fir. Additional tests have shown that the red heartwood of hickory is just as strong and serviceable as the white sap wood. Formerly, the custom has been to throw away the heartwood as useless. This discovery greatly extends the use of our hickory supply.

Heretofore, the custom has been to season woods by drying them in the sun. This method of curing not only took a long time but also was wasteful and expensive. The forestry scientists and lumbermen have now improved the use of dry kilns and artificial systems of curing green lumber. Now more than thirty-five of the leading woods such as Douglas fir, southern yellow pine, spruce, gum and oak can be seasoned in the kilns in short time. It used to take about two years of air drying to season fir and spruce. At present the artificial kiln performs this job in from twenty to forty days. The kiln-dried lumber is just as strong and useful for construction as the air-cured stock. Tests have proved that kiln drying of walnut for use in gun stocks or airplane propellers, in some cases reduced the waste of material from 60 to 2 per cent. The kiln-dried material was ready for use in one-third the time it would have taken to season the material in the air. Heavy green oak timbers for wagons and wheels were dried in the kiln in ninety to one hundred days. It would have taken two years to cure this material outdoors.

By their valuable test work, scientists are devising efficient means of protecting wood against decay. They treat the woods with such chemicals as creosote, zinc chloride and other preservatives. The life of the average railroad tie is at least doubled by such treatment. We could save about one and one-half billion board feet of valuable hardwood lumber annually if all the 85,000,000 untreated railroad ties now in use could be protected in this manner. If all wood exposed to decay were similarly treated, we could save about six billion board feet of timber each year.

About one-sixth of all the lumber that is cut in the United States is used in making crates and packing boxes. The majority of these boxes are not satisfactory. Either they are not strong enough or else they are not the right size or shape. During a recent year, the railroads paid out more than $100,000,000 to shippers who lost goods in transit due to boxes and crates that were damaged in shipment.

In order to find out what woods are best to use in crates and boxes and what sizes and shapes will withstand rough handling, the Laboratory experts developed a novel drum that tosses the boxes to and fro and gives them the same kind of rough handling they get on the railroad. This testing machine has demonstrated that the proper method of nailing the box is of great importance. Tests have shown that the weakest wood properly nailed into a container is more serviceable than the strongest wood poorly nailed. Better designs of boxes have been worked out which save lumber and space and produce stronger containers.

Educating the lumbering industry away from extravagant practices is one of the important activities of the modern forestry experts. Operators who manufacture handles, spokes, chairs, furniture, toys and agricultural implements could, by scientific methods of wood using, produce just as good products by using 10 to 50 per cent. of the tree as they do by using all of it.

The furniture industry not infrequently wastes from 40 to 60 per cent. of the raw lumber which it buys. Much of this waste could be saved by cutting the small sizes of material directly from the log instead of from lumber. It is also essential that sizes of material used in these industries be standardized.

The Forest Products Laboratory has perfected practical methods of building up material from small pieces which otherwise would be thrown away. For example, shoe lasts, hat blocks, bowling pins, base-ball bats, wagon bolsters and wheel hubs are now made of short pieces of material which are fastened together with waterproof glue. If this method of built-up construction can be made popular in all sections of the country, very great savings in our annual consumption of wood can be brought about. As matters now stand, approximately 25 per cent. of the tree in the forest is lost or wasted in the woods, 40 per cent. at the mills, 5 per cent. in seasoning the lumber and from 5 to 10 per cent. in working the lumber over into the manufactured articles. This new method of construction which makes full use of odds and ends and slabs and edgings offers a profitable way to make use of the 75 per cent. of material which now is wasted.

The vast importance of preserving our forests is emphasized when one stops to consider the great number of uses to which wood is put. In addition to being used as a building material, wood is also manufactured into newspaper and writing paper. Furthermore, it is a most important product in the making of linoleum, artificial silk, gunpowder, paints, soaps, inks, celluloid, varnishes, sausage casings, chloroform and iodoform. Wood alcohol, which is made by the destructive distillation of wood, is another important by-product. Acetate of lime, which is used extensively in chemical plants, and charcoal, are other products which result from wood distillation. The charcoal makes a good fuel and is valuable for smelting iron, tin and copper, in the manufacture of gunpowder, as an insulating material, and as a clarifier in sugar refineries.

It is predicted that the future fuel for use in automobile engines will be obtained from wood waste. Ethyl or "grain" alcohol can now be made from sawdust and other mill refuse. One ton of dry Douglas fir or southern yellow pine will yield from twenty to twenty-five gallons of 95 per cent. alcohol. It is estimated that more than 300,000,000 gallons of alcohol could be made annually from wood now wasted at the mills. This supply could be increased by the use of second-growth, inferior trees and other low-grade material.

CHAPTER XVIII

WOOD FOR THE NATION

Westward the course of forest discovery and depletion has taken its way in the United States. The pine and hardwood forests of the Atlantic and New England States first fell before the bite of the woodman's ax and the sweep of his saw. Wasteful lumbering finally sapped the resources of these productive timberlands. Shift was then made farther westward to the Lake States. Their vast stretches of white pine and native hardwoods were cut to a skeleton of their original size. The lumbering operations then spread to the southern pine belt. In a few years the supplies of marketable lumber in that region were considerably reduced. Then the westward trail was resumed. The strip of country between the Mississippi River and the Cascade, Sierra Nevada and Coast Ranges was combed and cut. Today, the last big drive against our timber assets is being waged in the forests of the Pacific Coast.

Our virgin forests originally covered 822,000,000 acres. Today, only one-sixth of them are left. All the forest land now in the United States including culled, burned and cut-over tracts, totals 463,000,000 acres. We now have more waste and cut-over lands in this country than the combined forest area of Germany, Belgium, Denmark, Holland, France, Switzerland,

Spain and Portugal. The merchantable timber left in the United States is estimated at 2,215,000,000,000 board feet. The rest is second-growth trees of poor quality. One-half of this timber is in California, Washington and Oregon. It is a long and costly haul from these Pacific Coast forests to the eastern markets. Less than one-fifth of our remaining timber is hardwood. 56,000,000,000 board feet of material of saw timber size are used or destroyed in the United States each year. Altogether, we use more than 26,000,000,000 cubic feet of timber of all classes annually. Our forests are making annual growth at the rate of less than one-fourth of this total consumption. We are rapidly cutting away the last of our virgin forests. We also are cutting small-sized and thrifty trees much more rapidly than we can replace them.

The United States is short on timber today because our fathers and forefathers abused our forests. If they had planted trees on the lands after the virgin timber was removed, we should now be one of the richest countries in the world in forest resources. Instead, they left barren stretches and desolate wastes where dense woods once stood. It is time that the present owners of the land begin the reclamation of our 326,000,000 acres of cut-over timberlands. Some of these lands still are yielding fair crops of timber due to natural restocking and proper care. Most of them are indifferent producers. One-quarter of all this land is bare of forest growth. It is our duty as citizens of the United States to aid as we may in the reforestation of this area.

Fires are cutting down the size of our forests each year. During a recent five-year period, 160,000 forest fires burned over 56,488,000 acres, an area as large as the state of Utah, and destroyed or damaged timber and property valued at $85,715,000. Year by year, fires and bad timber practices have been increasing our total areas of waste and cut-over land. We are facing a future lumber famine, not alone because we have used up our timber, but also because we have failed to make use of our vast acreage of idle land adapted for growing forests. We must call a halt and begin all over again. Our new start must be along the lines of timber planting and tree increase. The landowners, the States and the Federal Government must all get together in this big drive for reforestation.

It is impossible to make National Forests out of all the idle forest land. On the other hand, the matter of reforestation cannot be left to private owners. Some of them would set out trees and restore the forests as desired. Others would not. The public has large interests at stake. It must bear part of the burden. Proper protection of the forests against fire can come only through united public action. Everyone must do his part to reduce the fire danger. The public must also bring about needed changes in many of our tax methods so that private owners will be encouraged to go into the business of raising timber. The Government must do its share, the private landowner must help to the utmost and the public must aid in every possible way, including payment of higher prices for lumber as the cost of growing timber increases.

France and Scandinavia have solved their forest problems along about the same lines the United States will have to follow. These countries keep up well-protected public forests. All the landowners are taught how to set out and raise trees. Everyone has learned to respect the timberlands. The woods are thought of as treasures which must be carefully handled. The average man would no more think of abusing the trees in the forest than he would of setting fire to his home. The foreign countries are now busy working out their forestry problems of the years to come. We in America are letting the future take care of itself.

Our States should aid generally in the work of preventing forest fires. They should pass laws which will require more careful handling of private forest lands. They should pass more favorable timber tax laws so that tree growing will be encouraged. Uncle Sam should be the director in charge of all this work. He should instruct the states how to protect their forests against fire. He should teach them how to renew their depleted woodlands. He should work for a gradual and regular expansion of the National Forests. The United States Forest Service should have the power to help the various states in matters of fire protection, ways of cutting forests, methods of renewing forests and of deciding whether idle lands were better adapted for farming or forestry purposes.

Experts believe that the Government should spend at least $2,000,000 a year in the purchase of new National Forests. About one-fifth of all our forests are now publicly owned. One of the best ways of preventing the concentration of timber in private ownership is to increase the area of publicly owned forests. Such actions would prevent the waste of valuable timber and would aid planting work. For best results, it is thought that the Federal Government should own about one-half of all the forests in the country. To protect the watersheds of navigable streams the Government should buy 1,000,000 acres of woodlands in New England and 5,000,000 acres in the southern Appalachian Mountains. The National Forests should also be extended and consolidated.

Federal funds should be increased so that the Forest Service can undertake on a large scale the replanting of burned-over lands in the National Forests. As soon as this work is well under way, Congress should supply about $1,000,000 annually for such work. Many watersheds in the National Forests are bare of cover due to forest fires. As a result, the water of these streams is not sufficient for the needs of irrigation, water power and city water supply of the surrounding regions.

Right now, even our leading foresters do not know exactly what the forest resources of the country amount to. It will take several years to make such a survey even after the necessary funds are provided. We need to know just how much wood of each class and type is available. We want to know, in each case, the present and possible output. We want to find out the timber requirements of each state and of every important wood-using industry. Exact figures are needed on the timber stands and their growth. The experimental work of the Forest Service should be extended. Practically every forest is different from every other forest. It is necessary to work out locally the problems of each timber reservation. Most urgent of all is the demand for a law to allow Federal officers to render greater assistance to the state forestry departments in fighting forest fires.

Many state laws designed to perpetuate our forests must be passed if our remaining timber resources are to be saved. During times when fires threaten, all the forest lands in each state should be guarded by organized agencies. This protection should include cut-over and unimproved land as well as timber tracts. Such a plan would require that the State and Federal governments bear about one-half the expenses while the private forest owners should stand the balance. There would be special rules regulating the disposal of slashings, methods of cutting timber, and of extracting forest products such as pulpwood or naval stores.

If our forests are to be saved for the future we must begin conservation at once. To a small degree, luck plays a part in maintaining the size of the forest. Some woodlands in the South Atlantic States are now producing their third cut of saw logs. Despite forest fires and other destructive agencies, these forests have continued to produce. Some of the northern timber-lands have grown crops of saw timber and wood pulp for from one hundred fifty to two hundred fifty years. Expert foresters report that private owners are each year increasing their plantings on denuded woodlands. New England landowners are planting between 12,000,000 and 15,000,000 young forest trees a year. The Middle Atlantic and Central States are doing about as well. To save our forests, planting of this sort must be universal. It takes from fifty to one hundred years to grow a crop of merchantable timber. What the United States needs is a national forestry policy which will induce every landowner to plant and grow more trees on land that is not useful for farm crops. Our forestry problem is to put to work millions of acres of idle land. As one eminent forester recently remarked, "If we are to remain a nation of timber users, we must become a nation of wood growers."

Choose from Thousands of 1stWorldLibrary Classics By

Adolphus WilliamWard
Aesop
Agatha Christie
Alexander Aaronsohn
Alexander Kielland
Alexandre Dumas
Alfred Gatty
Alfred Ollivant
Alice Duer Miller
Alice Turner Curtis
Alice Dunbar
Ambrose Bierce
Amelia E. Barr
Andrew Lang
Andrew McFarland Davis
Anna Sewell
Annie Besant
Annie Hamilton Donnell
Annie Payson Call
Anton Chekhov
Arnold Bennett
Arthur Conan Doyle
Arthur Ransome
Atticus
B. M. Bower
Basil King
Bayard Taylor
Ben Macomber
Booth Tarkington
Bram Stoker
C. Collodi
C. E. Orr
C. M. Ingleby
Carolyn Wells
Catherine Parr Traill
Charles A. Eastman
Charles Dickens
Charles Dudley Warner
Charles Farrar Browne
Charles Ives
Charles Kingsley
Charles Lathrop Pack
Charles Whibley
Charles Willing Beale
Charlotte M. Braeme
Charlotte M.Yonge
Clair W. Hayes
Clarence Day Jr.
Clarence E. Mulford

Clemence Housman
Confucius
Cornelis DeWitt Wilcox
Cyril Burleigh
D. H. Lawrence
Daniel Defoe
David Garnett
Don Carlos Janes
Donald Keyhole
Dorothy Kilner
Dougan Clark
E. Nesbit
E.P.Roe
E. Phillips Oppenheim
Edgar Allan Poe
Edgar Rice Burroughs
Edith Wharton
Edward J. O'Biren
John Cournos
Edwin L. Arnold
Eleanor Atkins
Elizabeth Cleghorn
Gaskell
Elizabeth Von Arnim
Ellem Key
Emily Dickinson
Erasmus W. Jones
Ernie Howard Pie
Ethel Turner
Ethel Watts Mumford
Eugenie Foa
Eugene Wood
Evelyn Everett-Green
Everard Cotes
F. J. Cross
Federick Austin Ogg
Ferdinand Ossendowski
Francis Bacon
Francis Darwin
Frances Hodgson Burnett
Frank Gee Patchin
Frank Harris
Frank Jewett Mather
Frank L. Packard
Frederick Trevor Hill
Frederick Winslow Taylor
Friedrich Kerst
Friedrich Nietzsche
Fyodor Dostoyevsky

Gabrielle E. Jackson
Garrett P. Serviss
Gaston Leroux
George Ade
Geroge Bernard Shaw
George Ebers
George Eliot
George MacDonald
George Orwell
George Tucker
George W. Cable
George Wharton James
Gertrude Atherton
Grace E. King
Grant Allen
Guillermo A. Sherwell
Gulielma Zollinger
Gustav Flaubert
H. A. Cody
H. B. Irving
H. G. Wells
H. H. Munro
H. Irving Hancock
H. Rider Haggard
H. W. C. Davis
Hamilton Wright Mabie
Hans Christian Andersen
Harold Avery
Harold McGrath
Harriet Beecher Stowe
Harry Houidini
Helent Hunt Jackson
Helen Nicolay
Hendy David Thoreau
Henrik Ibsen
Henry Adams
Henry Ford
Henry Frost
Henry James
Henry Jones Ford
Henry Seton Merriman
Henry Wadsworth
Longfellow
Henry W Longfellow
Herbert A. Giles
Herbert N. Casson
Herman Hesse
Homer
Honore De Balzac

Horace Walpole
Horatio Alger, Jr.
Howard Pyle
Howard R. Garis
Hugh Lofting
Hugh Walpole
Humphry Ward
Ian Maclaren
Israel Abrahams
J.G.Austin
J. Henri Fabre
J. M. Barrie
J. Macdonald Oxley
J. S. Knowles
J. Storer Clouston
Jack London
Jacob Abbott
James Allen
James Lane Allen
James Andrews
James Baldwin
James DeMille
James Joyce
James Oliver Curwood
James Oppenheim
James Otis
Jane Austen
Jens Peter Jacobsen
Jerome K. Jerome
John Burroughs
John F. Kennedy
John Gay
John Glasworthy
John Habberton
John Joy Bell
John Milton
John Philip Sousa
Jonathan Swift
Joseph Carey
Joseph Conrad
Joseph Jacobs
Julian Hawthrone
Julies Vernes
Justin Huntly McCarthy
Kakuzo Okakura
Kenneth Grahame
Kate Langley Bosher
L. A. Abbot
L. T. Meade
L. Frank Baum
Laura Lee Hope

Laurence Housman
Leo Tolstoy
Leonid Andreyev
Lewis Carroll
Lilian Bell
Lloyd Osbourne
Louis Tracy
Louisa May Alcott
Lucy Fitch Perkins
Lucy Maud Montgomery
Lydia Miller Middleton
Lyndon Orr
M. H. Adams
Margaret E. Sangster
Margaret Vandercook
Maria Edgeworth
Maria Thompson Daviess
Mariano Azuela
Marion Polk Angellotti
Mark Overton
Mark Twain
Mary Austin
Mary Cole
Mary Rowlandson
Mary Wollstonecraft
Shelley
Max Beerbohm
Myra Kelly
Nathaniel Hawthrone
O. F. Walton
Oscar Wilde
Owen Johnson
P.G.Wodehouse
Paul and Mable Thorn
Paul G. Tomlinson
Paul Severing
Peter B. Kyne
Plato
R. Derby Holmes
R. L. Stevenson
Rabindranath Tagore
Rahul Alvares
Ralph Waldo Emmerson
Rene Descartes
Rex E. Beach
Richard Harding Davis
Richard Jefferies
Robert Barr
Robert Frost
Robert Gordon Anderson
Robert L. Drake

Robert Lansing
Robert Michael Ballantyne
Robert W. Chambers
Rosa Nouchette Carey
Ross Kay
Rudyard Kipling
Samuel B. Allison
Samuel Hopkins Adams
Sarah Bernhardt
Selma Lagerlof
Sherwood Anderson
Sigmund Freud
Standish O'Grady
Stanley Weyman
Stella Benson
Stephen Crane
Stewart Edward White
Stijn Streuvels
Swami Abhedananda
Swami Parmananda
T. S. Ackland
The Princess Der Ling
Thomas A. Janvier
Thomas A Kempis
Thomas Anderton
Thomas Bailey Aldrich
Thomas Bulfinch
Thomas De Quincey
Thomas H. Huxley
Thomas Hardy
Thomas More
Thornton W. Burgess
U. S. Grant
Valentine Williams
Victor Appleton
Virginia Woolf
Walter Scott
Washington Irving
Wilbur Lawton
Wilkie Collins
Willa Cather
Willard F. Baker
William Makepeace
Thackeray
William W. Walter
Winston Churchill
Yei Theodora Ozaki
Young E. Allison
Zane Grey

9 781421 804156